# HEREFORDSHIRE
# RAILWAYS

WILLIAM H. SMITH

SUTTON PUBLISHING LIMITED

Sutton Publishing Limited
Phoenix Mill · Thrupp · Stroud
Gloucestershire · GL5 2BU

First published 1998

**British Library Cataloguing in Publication Data**
A catalogue record for this book is available from the
British Library.

ISBN 0-7509-1814-4

Typeset in 10/12 Perpetua.
Typesetting and origination by
Sutton Publishing Limited.
Printed in Great Britain by
Ebenezer Baylis, Worcester.

Title page photograph: Engineman Charlie Smith says a last goodbye to his favourite locomotive at Round Oak steelworks near Stourbridge, where it had been sent to be cut up in 1959. With Dick Trapp on the opposite shift, Charlie had charge of the 'Thunderer', as local people called the Golden Valley train, for many years. Charlie had served the railways in various capacities for forty-five years by the time he retired in 1956. Always absorbed in the job he was carrying out, Charlie once wrote to the GWR management at Swindon works suggesting improvements that, through his experience, he considered would make the '58XX' class 0–4–2Ts even better engines. He was pleased that it was possible for him to preserve the cabside number-plate which is missing in this photo.

# ACKNOWLEDGEMENTS

The author acknowledges with thanks the following groups and individuals for their help in the creation of this book: Hereford CRO; HMRS Photo Collection; NRM, York; Pendon Museum Photo Collection; 6000LA; Lens of Sutton; Edwin John, Photographer, Hereford; Keith Beddoes, John Boynton, Roger Carpenter, Cliff Carr, Richard Casserley, Rhodri Clark, Derek Clayton, Hugh Davies, Peter Davies, Derek Harrison, Martin Hatton, the late R.E. Lacy, Michael E.M. Lloyd, John Phillips, Eric Rawlings, Arthur Sankey, Paul Shannon, F.W. 'Tim' Shuttleworth, the late Revd David Tipper, Adrian Vaughan, Bryan Wilson, Sid Wilding, John Wilkinson and Gordon Wood.

# Contents

Introduction                                                    5

1. Hereford, Ross & Gloucester Railway                          9

2. The Worcester & Hereford Railway                            29

3. The Golden Valley Railway                                   43

4. The Shrewsbury & Hereford Railway                           53

5. Hereford, Hay & Brecon Railway                              89

6. Leominster & Kington Railway                                95

7. Newport, Abergavenny & Hereford Railway                    109

8. Worcester, Bromyard & Leominster Railway                   117

9. Other Railways                                             123

   Bibliography                                               128

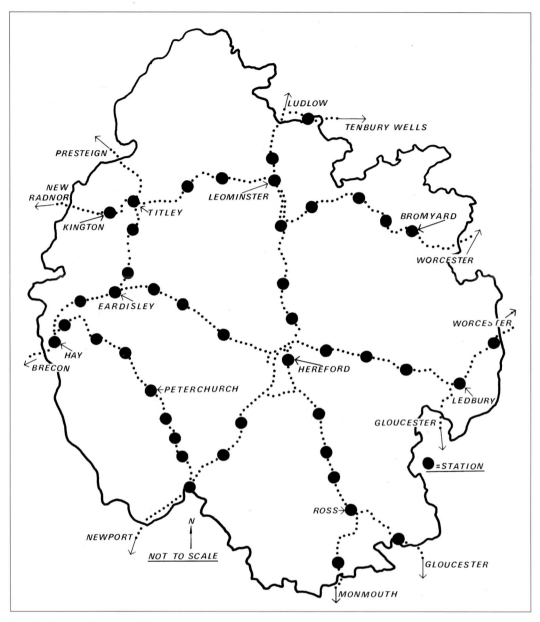

Herefordshire railways, *c.* 1902.

# INTRODUCTION

In the early years of the nineteenth century, Herefordshire's trading routes were oriented south-westwards towards the Bristol Channel and the Forest of Dean. Transport took two basic forms: navigation by barge, mainly on the River Wye; and haulage by horses, using stagecoaches, carriers' carts and laden packhorses. By these means, farm produce such as wool, cider and hops, along with timber and bark, were taken out of the county, and raw materials, coal and limestone in particular, were brought in.

At this time, coal from the Forest of Dean and from the Wyre Forest was being transported to meet a growing demand in Herefordshire for 'sale coal' at an economic price, for both the domestic hearth and the blacksmith's forge. Limestone in its various forms was used to surface roads, in the building trade, and latterly by farmers as a valued additive to the heavy clay soils that abound in in Herefordshire.

The canal age arrived in Herefordshire with the Kington, Leominster & Stourport Canal. This was an unsuccessful attempt to connect the limestone quarries near Kington with the Wyre Forest coalfield via Leominster, and from there to the River Severn.

In the first decade of the nineteenth century, the 'sale coal' industry was becoming important to the collieries of South Wales. This fuel was usually hauled by horse power along short feeder tramroads from the colliery to the nearest canal, from where it continued its journey. It was the development of three such tramroads that began Herefordshire's railway history. The Hay Railway opened in 1816 and was extended westwards in 1818; together with the Kington Railway of 1820 it offered 36 miles of horse-worked railway, bringing cheaper coal to the districts of West Herefordshire.

In 1829 the tramroad from Abergavenny reached Hereford, further reducing the cost of coal, and giving this trade from South Wales another boost. By 1836 a second railway boom was in full swing, following the establishment of the major English trunk routes. In 1838 the Gloucester Canal had been extended from Ledbury to Hereford. At that time, the authorized railways closest to the borders of Herefordshire were the Birmingham & Gloucester and the Taff Vale, both of which would play a connecting role in the later development of Herefordshire's railway map.

By 1845 boom had turned to 'mania', and Brunel's broad gauge developments had reached as far as Gloucester and were waiting parliamentary sanction to strike out through Ross and Hereford, and then north to Merseyside. By 1846 railways were well proven practically, and financially they appeared a sound investment; however, of the massive 560 railway-related bills submitted to parliament in 1846, fewer than half were favoured with Royal Assent. Among the failures was the Midland Welsh Railway, which considered Herefordshire only as a route to South Wales rather than as likely to create traffic from within the sparsely populated and unindustrialized county. Similarly Brunel's unsuccessful attempt in 1845 to tap the valuable Irish mail trade by connecting Worcester by rail with a harbour on the Lleyn Peninsula would have been routed via Leominster, Kington and Mid-Wales had it succeeded.

Among the railways that parliament did sanction in 1846 was the Shrewsbury & Hereford, but by this time railway construction was being held up by a national financial crisis which so depressed investment capital that work did not start on this line until 1850. Likewise, the Newport, Abergavenny & Hereford Railway, which received Royal Assent on the same day as the S&HR, remained in abeyance until the LNWR threw its weight behind it in 1851, eventually concluding a running agreement.

By December 1853, enjoying the notoriety of being the last English cathedral city to be connected to the nation's rail network, Hereford contained two stations. Barton (earlier referred to as Eign station) was the headquarters of the NA&HR, while the S&HR's terminus was no more than a platform close to a mansion called Barrs Court at the lower end of what is now College Road. These two termini were not directly connected, although they were linked from a junction to the north of the S&HR station by a mile-long line known as the 'Worcester mile'. This was owned by a third company, the Worcester & Hereford Railway, which was ready to run into the NA&HR's Barton station.

The 'Worcester mile' became vital at a later date, particularly to the LNWR, since it represented their gateway to the Monmouthshire coalfield. Gaining access to South Wales via Herefordshire, both through Shrewsbury and via Worcester, was a high priority for the newly evolved LNWR, which is why it backed (jointly with the Midland Railway) the Worcester & Hereford Railway.

Until a Parliamentary Committee report put a brake on the process, the 1850s saw a period of amalgamation and absorption of small local railway companies, leading to the growth of the GWR, among others. London could be reached from Hereford via Gloucester once the Hereford Ross & Gloucester Railway opened the broad gauge line to the barely completed Barrs Court station on 1 June 1855. The S&HR entered into a joint agreement with the HR&GR to share the organization of the station with its mixed gauge lines.

In 1862, a great amount of time was spent in parliament and in the boardrooms of the respective companies ironing out the issue of running powers and leasing arrangements on the S&HR, until this was settled in July 1862 by sharing them out between the LNWR, West Midland Railway and GWR, the latter progressing to become joint owners (with the LNWR) when they absorbed the WMR in August 1863. The GWR thereby acquired the W&HR through the WMR constituent, gaining control of a route for which the LNWR and MR previously had ambitions. The NA&HR also came to the GWR under the umbrella of the WMR consortium, having earlier fallen out with its original supporters, the LNWR. The HR&GR was also amalgamated with the GWR in 1862.

The two main players on the Herefordshire railway scene for the following forty years were established in 1863, although the MR also played a role during this period. The LNWR had become isolated at Barrs Court station – a dead end for their services – so to remedy this, on 16 July 1866 the LNWR opened a loop from the GWR's Newport route at Red Hill to Rotherwas Junction on the Gloucester line, from where the GWR added rails to form mixed gauge lines into Barrs Court station.

By means of an extension of their running powers from Shelwick Junction, MR goods trains started working into Barton from the W&HR line in 1868, to be followed by passenger services a year later. The MR then attained its ambition to connect with the South Wales coalfield by relieving the HH&BR of its continual financial struggles on 1 October 1869, at first using the minimal facilities at Hereford's third station at Moorfields, which involved complicated shunting movements and led to the MR's attempt to use Barton station instead. This took until 1874, when the GWR's opposition to the move was resolved in the MR's favour. The same year also saw the removal of the broad gauge line in Barrs Court station.

While developments were taking place in the city of Hereford, many of the county's gentry and landowners around the smaller Herefordshire market towns had been seeking to organize their own local branch line during the period when the major operators were establishing a new dimension in local transport. Every small town seemed to want a railway station, though a few shopkeepers were not so sure: they feared their trade would be drawn away to bigger towns. Like the many pipedreams of the 'mania' years, several local schemes failed to materialize, and those that did experienced funding difficulties.

In 1878, the Mayor and Corporation of Hereford complained to the Board of Trade about poor station accommodation in the city. The GWR/LNWR, in a Joint Committee report, recommended the development of Barton with the MR's financial help. The MR rejected the conditions, so Barrs Court station was not improved until 1883.

By late Victorian times, railway traffic through Herefordshire had greatly increased, assisted in particular by the opening of the Severn Tunnel on 1 September 1886 and by the abandonment of the broad gauge line west of Exeter in May 1892. The construction in 1893 of two curved loops to the north of Barrs Court station meant that MR trains started to use Barrs Court instead of Barton, which became redundant.

The 1896 Light Railways Act was intended to encourage the development of public rail transport in rural districts, and although several schemes were proposed, there was no response to the encouragement in Herefordshire.

By the turn of the century, the GWR had breathed life into the Golden Valley line, and had secured the long-delayed Bromyard through route from Leominster to Worcester. The MR established through carriages on trains between Birmingham and

Swansea via Hereford. By the Edwardian era, employment as a railwayman had become a major source of income in Herefordshire, and carried with it prestige and security second to none.

The First World War, when the nation's railways came under government control, saw Herefordshire's main lines being used to transport coal from South Wales in exceptionally heavy trains known as 'Jellicoe specials' to fuel the Royal Navy's fleet. Rotherwas and Credenhill were chosen as rail-linked ammunition factory sites, the GWR's Eardisley branch closed for a time, and women were employed on railway work as manpower became short.

The grouping of 1922 meant that the LMS took over the duties previously carried out by the LNWR and MR in Herefordshire. The railwaymen of Herefordshire were involved in industrial disputes before and after the First World War, culminating in the General Strike. Of the many changes taking place in the late 1920s, the most significant to the railways was the onset of the rapid development of local bus services and motorized transport in general.

The LMS cut back the goods traffic on the old Midland line in the 1930s, having dispensed with the Moorfields engine shed in 1924. The ex-LNWR shed closed in 1938, and both sheds' locomotives were transferred to Barton shed.

GWR main line traffic showed little decline in the 1930s, and as in the previous war, Herefordshire routes were vital pathways between 1939 and 1945. Rotherwas, Moreton on Lugg and Pontrilas were rail-connected MoD sites of strategic significance that arose from wartime needs.

The run-down post-war railways battled against further increases in competition from private motoring, shortages and poor-quality coal. The change to a nationalized system in 1948 meant that all of Herefordshire's lines came under the control of British Railways Western Region by 1950. The Eardisley–Kington line was a wartime casualty, as was the Golden Valley passenger route, and in the 1950s Leominster–Bromyard (all services) and the passenger trains on the Leominster–Kington line were lost for ever.

The 1960s brought wholesale closures to what remained of the rail system in Herefordshire as a result of the Beeching Reports of 1963 and 1965, and Herefordshire was eventually left with Barrs Court, Leominster and Ledbury stations as the only halts for the new diesel trains. At this point it appeared that rail freight would be completely superseded by road haulage, leaving a small parcel and mail business as the only non-passenger remnant.

The 1970s were entered with a great amount of pessimism that the line north of Shelwick Junction might be closed. However, extended passenger services beyond Crewe and Cardiff brought in more custom, and between 1984 and 1987 a reversal in fortunes occurred on the North & West line through Herefordshire, while the Ledbury route, singled in 1984, is still open, so, given the resurgence in rail freight traffic as a result of the expansive policy of the EWS Railway following privatization, the opportunities for photographing the various aspects of the railways of Herefordshire look good for a while yet.

# CHAPTER ONE

# HEREFORD, ROSS & GLOUCESTER RAILWAY

*A GWR broad gauge 0–6–0 on a gauge conversion train stands at Grange Court, about to proceed towards Ross and Hereford, August 1869. This collection of vehicles consisted of vans providing sleeping accommodation, a travelling office for engineers, smiths' shops, stores and temporary kitchens, and came to be based at Hereford. A total of 21½ miles of single track were converted to narrow gauge in five days. Disc and crossbar signals and a fantail signal typical of the period are visible behind the engine. The men are standing on the crossbar, and are holding on to the disc for support. (E. John Collection)*

Isambard Kingdom Brunel surveyed a route for a Gloucester, Ross & Hereford Railway in the 1830s. His intention was to construct a strategically placed broad gauge branch to his anticipated Cheltenham & Great Western Union Railway. If Hereford could be connected via Gloucester, Brunel saw the possibility of constructing a broad gauge route all the way from South Wales via Shrewsbury to Birkenhead and the north-west. However, neither this nor any of the other six proposals in the mid-1840s, narrow or broad gauge, achieved their ambitions to link Hereford and Gloucester by train.

Brunel attended a public meeting at the Shirehall, Hereford, on 30 December 1850, where assurances of financial support that had previously been lacking were given for a plan to route a broad gauge railway from Gloucester via Grange Court to Hereford, resurrecting the main part of a scheme for a Monmouth & Hereford Railway that had been aborted in 1845 and which became the foundation of the Hereford, Ross & Gloucester Railway Company, incorporated in June 1851.

Rapid parliamentary ratification of the HR&GR was followed by delays in construction, so by 1853 only the first 5 miles of the total 22½ miles of single broad gauge line had opened from Grange Court to a temporary station at Hopesbrook near Longhope.

The year 1853 was a disappointing one for Brunel's broad gauge empire. Parliament rejected plans for both the Shrewsbury & Hereford broad gauge line and the proposed mixed gauge Worcester & Hereford, thereby thwarting Brunel's ambitions for the HR&GR to become an essential link in his extension plans.

The remainder of the line to Hereford from Hopesbrook, including four tunnels and four timber-built river crossings, took two more years to complete, and opened on 1 June 1855, worked by the GWR. In Hereford, the HR&GR ran partly over mixed gauge track within Barrs Court station, under the supervision of a Joint Committee with the Shrewsbury & Hereford Railway Company.

As enthusiasm for broad gauge evaporated, a decision was made by the HR&GR to organize a major logistical exercise to convert the HR&GR line between Grange Court and Rotherwas Junction to standard gauge. Amazingly, this was achieved in less than a week during August 1869. The popularity of the scenic Wye Valley with the Victorian travelling classes and ample traffic based on agricultural goods and merchandise kept the line economical and busy through to the 1890s, and to a slightly lesser degree, into the new century up until the First World War.

In 1917, the choice of Rotherwas for the site of a rail-linked Royal Ordnance Factory brought with it a major increase in the line's traffic. The factory employed many young women from the surrounding districts, and both early and late shift 'workgirl specials' were worked into Rotherwas from Ross as well as from Hereford. This pattern was later repeated during the Second World War, and an extensive internal railway layout developed inside the security fences. A workman's train to Rotherwas from Ross was still in operation in October 1947.

By the 1930s, public then private road traffic competition had inevitably affected the line's income. Station receipts at Ross in 1938 were down to almost half the peak 1923 figure, and lower than 1903's takings. August Bank Holiday excursion traffic of 1939 took trains to places such as Paignton, while cattle traffic was still heavy enough to require the rostering of 2–6–0 '26XX' class locomotives for haulage.

The Hereford–Gloucester line had been so well engineered that it was possible for it to carry heavily loaded trains not just in wartime emergencies, but in peacetime, too. It was frequently used as a convenient by-pass for the North & West main line trains during engineering operations or other problems on that line. Often on a Sunday, long-distance expresses double-headed by a pilot engine and any 4–6–0 except the 'King' class could be seen working via the HR&GR. The through coaches from Hereford to Paddington via Gloucester ceased to run during the Second World War, and in spite of their later reinstatement by BR(W) in 1948 and the restoration of something resembling the pre-war passenger timetable with eight Gloucester and Hereford trains each way, the traffic decline continued, on both local and longer-distance services.

In the 1950s, increasing car ownership led to a further fall in demand by passengers, and this plus the bus competition eventually led to the complete closure of the Hereford–Gloucester passenger service in November 1964, accompanied by the closure of the Hereford–Ross section. Goods traffic alone could not keep the line economically viable, and only a year later the remaining section of the line to Gloucester was closed, too.

## The Ross & Monmouth Railway

Like many towns of its size, Monmouth appeared in numerous mid-nineteenth-century prospectuses for grandiose but unfulfilled railway schemes. Most of these schemes would have placed Monmouth on major through routes.

The rail link into Herefordshire was finally completed when the Ross & Monmouth Railway (incorporated by Acts in 1865 and 1867) was officially opened to Monmouth (May Hill) on 1 August 1873, extending to Troy station in May 1874. The gauge conversion of the HR&GR enabled a standard gauge junction with that railway to be constructed. Although worked by the GWR from the start, the R&MR remained a nominally independent company until 1922, when it was absorbed into the GWR, the Monmouth Company still producing a working profit.

Like its neighbour, the HR&GR, the line had its heyday at the time of the late Victorian excursions to Tintern, Symonds Yat and the Wye Valley. Timber, stone and farm produce provided some freight, but this traffic was never substantial. Walford Halt and Kerne Bridge station were sited within the county boundary of Herefordshire.

The Ross–Monmouth line lost its passenger services on 5 January 1959, accompanied by celebratory champagne for the footplate crew, and the Ross Town Band on the platform at Ross playing 'Auld Lang Syne'. Freight continued to run for a short time as far as Lydbrook Junction, the section beyond that being closed with the withdrawal of the Monmouth passenger trains, then this service ceased on 1 November 1965.

Ex-GWR '14XX' 0–4–2T produces a surfeit of steam in the Monmouth Branch bay at Ross-on-Wye station, c. 1953. The train is the autocoach service to Monmouth. (Rawlins)

Ex-GWR 33XX 'Bulldog' class 4–4–0 No. 3455 *Starling* at Barrs Court station, having arrived on a stopping passenger train from Gloucester, 9 September 1949 – a familiar task for the few remaining members of the class at the time, based at either Hereford or Gloucester sheds. No. 3455 was withdrawn in June 1950, the last in building sequence of the 'Birds', which included modifications such as much deeper frames around the trailing axleboxes. (H.C. Casserley)

An ex-MSWJR 4–4–0 built by the North British Railway Company, absorbed by the GWR and renumbered No. 1123, seen here at the south end of Barrs Court station, 1936. It was typical for Gloucester trains to arrive at this platform, and as No. 1123 was shedded at Gloucester for a period during 1936, it is safe to assume that this is a stopping train to Gloucester via Ross-on-Wye. (HMRS)

A view of the goods shed at Ross on Wye, *c*. 1955. (Rawlings)

Ross-on-Wye Up Home bracket signal, *c*. 1955. This signal protected Ross station from the Hereford direction. The left-hand arm related to the Up Main to Up Sidings route, while the centre was the Up Main Home. The right-hand arm with two holes was a backing signal that controlled routes via the Down Main line to the loading dock, for instance. (Rawlings)

Ross station, *c.* 1892. This view shows the road approach to Ross station from the south-west after the new building opened in 1892, replacing an earlier building dating from the broad gauge days. The original South signal-box, closed in 1938, can be seen beyond the Monmouth branch bay on the far right. (E. John Collection)

A Gloucester–Hereford train enters the Down platform at Ross station, *c.* 1910. It may be a special train, judging by the appearance of the waiting passengers. The train engine is a GWR Dean '2301' class 0–6–0, its shiny brass dome being typical of the Edwardian appearance of GWR locomotives. The tender is, even at this date, already elderly, being of double-framed design.

The station staff at Ross, *c*. 1895. The only item of uniform worn by the station master (sitting, centre) is the stiff-sided peaked cap with gold-braided peak and a gilt wreath around the GWR initials. Office workers (sitting) were not issued with uniform. Porters were dressed in green corduroy, wearing sleeved waistcoats in summer; an identification number appeared on their armband. The young man on the extreme right merits a uniform denoting his superiority by its stand-up collar and his grade written on the front of his cap. The presence of a stretcher may signify the staff's success in an inter-station first aid competition which the company frequently organized. (Maggs Collection)

Webb, Hall and Webb Ltd and Samuel Llewellyn and Son were two local coal merchants at Ross-on-Wye in the early 1950s who received their coal supplies for domestic use by goods train. In this view, *c.* 1954, Ross-on-Wye goods yard is seen from the south-west, looking towards the goods shed.

A GWR 2–4–0 at the Hereford end of Ross station reverses its train under close scrutiny of railway officials, 29 October 1900. The Duke and Duchess of York had visited Monmouth, and were due to board the special train. In view are the goods shed, the original North signal-box and a privately owned wagon belonging to a local Ross merchant, Samuel Llewellyn and Son. (Maggs Collection)

Ross station, looking towards Gloucester and the engine shed, 1919. An end loading bay is seen on the right, originally to assist the transport of a family horse carriage on a flat wagon attached to a train. The track from the right gave direct trailing connections between the goods shed and both Up and Down lines. Ground signals protected the access. The water column was essential to supply small tank engines on through goods trains. The sheeted wagons in the sidings to the left are probably transporting hay.

Ex-GWR '43XX' Class 2–6–0 No. 7335 brings a Gloucester–Hereford train into Ross-on-Wye, *c.* 1958. The fireman is about to surrender the token to the Ross signalman standing on the platform ramp. The signal-box opened in 1938, a single box replacing the previous South and North boxes. (E.T. Rawlins)

Ex-GWR '51XX' Class 2–6–2T No. 4124 pauses at Ross-on-Wye station on its journey from Gloucester to Hereford in the summer of 1964, the engine usually provided by Cheltenham sub-shed for this duty. Since the line's closure, the words 'Change for Monmouth' have been removed from the platform running-in board; the 'on-Wye' suffix was not added by the GWR until 1933, as a ploy to attract more tourist traffic. At the time of the photograph, even small ex-GWR locos like this Prairie tank were being painted in Brunswick Green with orange/black lining. No. 4124 was withdrawn from Worcester shed in August 1964.

GWR 'Duke' class 4–4–0 No. 3289 of Gloucester shed brings a stopping train into Ross in June 1939. The 4–4–0 locos were the main type used on Hereford–Gloucester passenger trains in the 1930s. The train includes the through coach to Hereford off the prestigious 'Cheltenham Flyer', which brought Ross to within three hours and five minutes of London. The Monmouth branch autocoach stands awaiting its next duty; a wagonload of 'loco' coal is in front of the locomotive shed on the right. (R. Carpenter Collection)

Ross-on-Wye station, looking towards Hereford, *c.* 1955. The Monmouth branch passenger trains used the bay to the left of the photograph. The turnout released the train engine, allowing it to run around its carriages. This fell out of use after the allocation of autotrains to the route. The track was lifted in 1963. The Ross goods yard crane can be seen beyond the buffer stop.

Rotherwas Junction signal-box opened in 1917, replacing a previous box there since 1880. This view looks south towards Dinedor Hill, September 1964, the month the box was taken out of use, and two months before the line between the junction and Ross closed. The line to Gloucester is to the left. The double track to the far right is the cut-off loop line constructed by the LNWR and opened in July 1866. The flat ground beyond this curve is occupied by sewage works lying inside a long meander of the River Wye through Lower Bullingham. The track immediately to the right of the box led to the complex group of sidings that served the Rotherwas Royal Ordnance Factory, originally built for the Ministry of Munitions in 1916–17. (Blencowe)

Holme Lacy station, looking towards Ross-on-Wye, c. 1920. The single platform with passing loop was constructed within a cutting. The garden regularly won prizes in GWR inter-station competitions, and in 1927 the judges wrote of the high bank massed with yellow Rose of Sharon mingled with red roses. (Author's Collection)

Holme Lacy station, *c.* 1920. A GWR 0–6–0PT starts its train towards Ross, while a GWR 0–6–0ST waits in the loop with a goods train. Traffic in cord timber from local woodlands around Woolhope is much in evidence, as demand for its use as pit-props was high at the time. The signal-box was taken out of use in 1925, and replaced by two groundframes. (Author's Collection)

A Gloucester-bound passenger train with Gloucester shed's ex-GWR '63XX' class 2–6–0 No. 6304 in charge passes through Holme Lacy station, late summer 1963. The train has just left the 110 yd long Dinedor tunnel to the north. The photograph shows dumped scrap where prize-winning gardens once grew. (A. Vickers)

Hereford shed's ex-GWR '2251' class Collett 0–6–0 No. 2242 heads a Gloucester-bound train at Ballingham station, looking north towards the 1206 yd long Ballingham tunnel, early 1960s. The station was a late addition to the Hereford–Gloucester route, opening on 1 September 1908 with a siding loop controlled by two groundframes.

The pagoda-style waiting hut at Backney Halt between Fawley and Ross-on-Wye was opened on 17 July 1933. Seen here in BR days, a pulley system was in use to avoid the need to climb up a ladder to the station illuminations.

Fawley station, looking towards Hereford and Fawley tunnel (537 yd), *c.* 1900. The railway from Hereford crossed the River Wye on Carey Viaduct to reach Fawley from Ballingham. Fawley was originally a single-platform station, later doubled. The wide space between the running lines shows evidence of the line's broad-gauge origin. The signal-box, which also controlled the station level-crossing, closed when traffic ceased on 2 November 1964. Until 20 October 1964, a small loop siding with cattle pens was available at the Hereford end of the station. Entry to this siding was controlled by a groundframe. (K. Beddoes Collection)

Gloucester shed's ex-GWR '43XX' class No. 7335 is Hereford-bound as it crosses with a passenger heading the other way, at Fawley station, *c.* 1961. At this time, the '43XX' class had a near monopoly of the passenger turns, whereas in September 1949 the 'Bulldog' class 4–4–0s from Hereford shed had this role. On 30 September 1949, No. 3455 *Starling* and No. 3401 *Vancouver* were noted on crossing trains at Fawley. (F.K. Davies)

Mitcheldean Road station, looking towards Gloucester, *c.* 1920. The addition of the word 'Road' to a GWR station should have warned unsuspecting passengers that the station was not actually in the immediate vicinity of the village it claimed to serve.

Mitcheldean Road station yard, *c.* 1910. Unloading of heavy machinery has almost been completed. The flat implement wagons from the Great Eastern Railway have wooden chocks on their decks. A boiler has yet to be unloaded. It is unclear what role the traction engine served; it may be part of the load.

A GWR '43XX' class 2–6–0 and brake van test the new section of Strangford Bridge, 8 September 1947. The bridge ha collapsed into the River Wye on 29 March 1947 as a result of damage by flood water following a rapid thaw of the dee snow cover of that month. In the intervening period, passenger trains ran from Hereford to Fawley, hauled by 0–4–2T and 0–6–0PTs. A bus service then connected travellers to Ross-on-Wye to continue their journey. The 7.05 a.m Hereford–Paddington was scheduled to start from Ross for the duration.

South Herefordshire Agricultural Co-operative Society, one of the main agricultural suppliers in the Ross-on-Wy district, had their own wagons. The two pictured here in the 1930s are typically transporting loads of root crops, possibl sugar beet. Ross-on-Wye cattle dock is in the background. (HMRS Collection)

Weston under Penyard Halt, 1953. Situated at 130 miles 21 chains between Mitcheldean Road and Ross-on-Wye stations, it was opened by the GWR on 2 December 1929 in an attempt to compete for passengers with local bus services. (E.T. Rawlins)

Ross-on-Wye shed, a sub-shed of Hereford, with ex-GWR '57XX' class 0–6–0PT No. 7705 inside, c. 1956. This class of loco worked the pick-up goods trains at this period. Ten years earlier, '48XX' class 0–4–2Ts Nos 4804 and 4845 were allocated for passenger work, along with '74XX' class 0–6–0PTs Nos 7416 and 7420 for Monmouth branch goods duties. In the siding, the Monmouth branch auto-trailer awaits its next trip. The shed was open by 1871 to service the Monmouth branch, but the arch above the entrance, which has subsequently been filled in, points to the design being of broad gauge era. (Photomatic)

A '517' class 0–4–2T stands in Ross station preparing to depart for Monmouth during the first decade of the twentieth-century. The branch passenger train between the two towns was nicknamed 'The Bullet'. In this view, the passenger accommodation consists of two carriages sandwiched between a full brake van for luggage and three horseboxes.

Kerne Bridge station, c. 1900. A '517' class 0–4–2T heads a passenger train towards the 634 yd Coppet Hill tunnel, and will cross the River Wye at this point on its way to Monmouth. An empty carriage truck brings up the rear of the four- or six-wheeled gas-lit carriages. The local carrier's horse and cart seen in the station approach used to meet all trains. 'For Goodrich Castle' was added to the station name-board to encourage tourist traffic, and a camping coach was situated here at a later date.

Ex-GWR Collett '2251' class 0–6–0 No. 2253 enters Ross-on-Wye with a freight train off the Monmouth branch, 1964. Following closure of their sub-shed in 1964, Ross-on-Wye crews continued to work the line, but with Hereford-based locos until the line to Lydbrook Junction closed on 1 November 1965.

Walford Halt, looking towards Kerne Bridge with the River Wye to the right, 10 July 1959. Opened on 23 February 1931, this was one of several halts constructed in the county around this time in an effort to counter the growing competition from bus companies. In 1955, an observer remarked: 'it should be replaced by a new halt where the Ross–Coleford road crosses the railway at which point there is a large and growing housing estate'. (H.C. Casserley)

A GWR '517' class 0–4–2T brings a train of clerestory coaches from Gloucester towards Ross out of Lea Line tunnel, *c.* 1910. The photo looks down into the cutting from the road bridge that became part of the A40 to Gloucester. The tall wooden post of the Mitcheldean Road distant signal is in the foreground. (R. Carpenter Collection)

Ex-GWR 0–4–2T No. 1406 heads towards Monmouth, 30 May 1952. The location is just outside Ross-on-Wye, close to Alton Court, once the site of a locally renowned brewery whose excellent beer was attributed partly to the nature of the local spring water. (E.R. Morten)

# CHAPTER TWO

# THE WORCESTER &
# HEREFORD RAILWAY

*Ashperton station, looking towards Stoke Edith and Shelwick Junction, c. 1956. In 1894, Ashperton was staffed by one inspector (i.e. a stationmaster), one porter and two signalmen. Prior to 1891, the signalman had assisted with platform duties, including supervising the weighing machine, but in that year the signal-box was moved away from the platform and the signalman worked a twelve-hour day confined to his box. As a result, weighing machine receipts fell, which the company blamed on the machine often being left unattended. A lad porter was thereafter employed at £26 p.a. to trim, clean and take out a total of thirty-four signal lamps, to assist generally, and to oversee the weighing machine in particular. Subsequently, an increased return of £7 from the weighing machine was noted at the end of 1893. In 1899, the GWR Engineering Committee agreed to the construction of new station buildings, verandas and a footbridge at an estimated cost of £1,600. Extra sidings were to be provided at the same time. The signal-box seen in the distance was closed on 25 October 1964.*

The first proposal to build a railway between Worcester and Hereford came at the height of the 'railway mania' in 1845. However, like two other schemes to link the cathedral cities which followed in 1846, the idea disappeared quite quickly, and did not resurface in public until 1851. In that year, at the direction of the Town Council, representatives from Worcester travelled to London to discuss possibilities with the LNWR directors. Finding a route to link their lines in the North and Midlands with South Wales was a burning ambition of both the LNWR and the MR, and as this could be achieved via Worcester and Hereford, both expressed interest in making a joint line, given enough local support.

In the autumn of 1852, agreement to subscribe to a W&HR by the LNWR, the MR and the Newport, Abergavenny & Hereford Railway immediately provoked combined opposition from the broad gauge practioners, and a rival plan to run on mixed gauge was produced.

Much parliamentary time was then taken up by the arguments of both factions, and plans of a preferred route altered within each camp. Eventually, the W&HR was incorporated on 15 August 1853, to run between Worcester (Tunnel Junction and Shrub Hill Junction) and Hereford (Shelwick Junction) as a narrow gauge railway just over 27 miles in length.

The engineering features required included two long viaducts, a bridge across the River Severn and three tunnels, so building the line was clearly going to be quite a feat. It was 1859 before traffic commenced, and then only between Henwick and Malvern Link; not until 1861 did the single-line section make its entry into Barrs Court, Hereford, and by then the company formed part of the amalgamated West Midland Railway. At this time the public travelling to London from Hereford through Worcester would arrive not at Paddington, but at Euston. They would have travelled via the LNWR's line through Bletchley.

By 1863, the WMR was swallowed up in turn by the GWR, which allowed the Midland Railway running powers to Hereford from Worcester. The W&HR route enters Herefordshire at the Colwall end of the 1,395 yd long first tunnel under the Malvern Hills, which proved extremely troublesome to construct and then maintain. A second replacement tunnel was opened through to Colwall in 1926. Still only a single-line passage was available, and the suggestion of renovating the original opening came to nothing. Another tunnel at Ledbury was a single line of narrow bore, and had such a gradient that for much of its life a banking engine had to be stationed at Ledbury.

From Ledbury, a branch to Gloucester was opened on 27 July 1885, finally closed completely as far as Dymock on 13 July 1959. Motive power on the line continued to be supplied by ex-West Midland Railway locomotives for some years after the demise of that company, and there is a record of ex-OWWR 2–4–0 No. 181 failing at Ashperton station on the 7.35 p.m. Worcester–Hereford passenger train as late as 1897. By the turn of the century, more modern GWR 2–4–0s of the '111' class were in use, to be joined at Hereford shed by other 2–4–0s of the '4816', '806' and '2201' classes. These locos were employed on the Worcester–Hereford trains connecting with Paddington expresses, as well as Birmingham–Cardiff stopping trains.

As the 2–4–0s wore out, the 4–4–0 classes, particularly William Dean's 'Bulldog' class, were to be found at Hereford shed for the Worcester line passenger duties. At this time, in the 1920s, 'Dean Goods' and 'Standard Goods' were predominant on local goods traffic, while the 'Aberdare' 2–6–0, '28XX' 2–8–0 and later 2–8–0 and 2–8–2 tank classes came to haul the long, heavy coal trains en route to the West Midlands from Pontypool Road.

The 4–4–0s began to be ousted in turn by 4–6–0s of the 'Hall' and 'Saint' classes, in particular on the South Wales passenger trains in the late 1930s – a trend which continued through the Second World War and until just after nationalization, when several 'Saint' class 4–6–0s ran their final trains on W&HR lines.

One of the first lines to see the use of the GWR's diesel railcars was the Hereford–Worcester line, when a service was introduced in 1935 between Hereford and Oxford, with a connection there to Paddington.

During the years when steam was fast disappearing, standard BR designs of the 9F 2–10–0 were in constant use on through freight trains, with passenger services enjoying the three-coach DMU units.

The line from Ledbury to the junction with the Shrewsbury & Hereford line at Shelwick was singled in 1984, but continued to provide a route for Hereford to London (Paddington) passenger services via Worcester and Oxford, including 'HST', 'Sprinter' and latterly 'Turbo' DMUs.

An early photograph at Withington looking towards Stoke Edith, possibly 1862. The locomotive is an ex-OWWR 0–6–0, owned at the time of the photograph by the WMR. It was built by Fairburn to a design identical to that used by Kirtley for the Midland Railway. The slotted signal is of interest, as are the so-called 'illiterate marks' branding the wagons on the left, allegedly to assist employees of the day to recognize company vehicles. The siding to the right behind the signal dives off at an interestingly sharp angle. (Ballard Collection, Hereford CRO)

Withington station, looking towards Stoke Edith, *c.* 1862. The single line was later doubled, but the sidings and goods shed are already *in situ*. Apart from the brick-built weighbridge office, the buildings are in the style of engineer Stephen Ballard's pre-fabricated wooden structures, probably some of the first using this method. (Ballard Collection, Hereford CRO)

Withington station, looking towards Hereford and the road overbridge, *c.* 1862. The WMR locomotive with a fluted steam dome is a 2–4–0 built by Messrs Wilson for the OWWR. The footplate crews are dressed in the typical white fustian uniform of the time, while the posing onlookers appear to include some other railway employees. (Ballard Collection, Hereford CRO)

Withington station, *c.* 1930. Withington was the home depot of Edwin Munslow, Weston House, coal, coke and lime merchant, whose privately owned wagons were once a familiar sight in the station sidings beyond the overbridge in this view towards Stoke Edith.

Withington station, looking towards Hereford, February 1958. By this time the Worcester–Hereford local steam trains had been taken over by three-coach DMUs such as the one seen entering the station. Steam locomotives still shunted and hauled the freight, and ex-GWR '2251' class 0–6–0 No. 2242 stands awaiting its next move in the sidings. In the background can be seen a kiln which was part of the Lugwardine Tile Works, to which a siding connected.

Signalman Fletcher inside Withington signal-box, c. 1925. This signal-box was classified by the GWR in 1914 as in the 'Principal Main Line' category, which entitled the signalman to a basic pay of 28s 6d per week at that time. Any goods train driver bound for Barton Yard was required to give one 'crow' on his whistle as his train passed Withington Box, so that the signalman could indicate to the next box at Shelwick Junction that the goods needed to be turned off the main line into Barton. The signal-box closed on 14 December 1964.

Stoke Edith station, looking towards Ashperton as a GWR 2–4–0 slows for the station stop with a train from the Worcester direction, *c.* 1910. The signals, signal-box and level crossing gate posts show the trademark finials of the manufacturer, Messrs MacKenzie and Holland, whose factory was at Worcester. The platform lamp has an unusual wooden base.

Stoke Edith station, looking towards Ashperton and Ledbury, 29 August 1960. The crossing gates were replaced by lifting barriers on 9 February 1973, and the signal-box remains in use to control them. The trackwork leading into the small goods shed on the Hereford side of the station was taken out of use in 1963, and the remaining sidings were out of use by 21 January 1973.

Stoke Edith station, *c.* 1912. It was normal for the GWR to provide antiquated four- and six-wheeled carriages with all the doors locked during the journey as 'hop-pickers' specials' to stations such as Stoke Edith which were situated within reach of hopyards. The carriage stock had once seen service on the London Metropolitan Underground lines, which can be detected from the rounded top to the carriage doors, which, if accidentally left open, would not catch on the tunnel walls. This train has arrived from the Black Country direction, source of much of the casual labour. This special is probably for friends and relatives paying a brief visit.

A young boy porter looks on bemused as the hop-pickers scramble on board with their baggage to begin the return journey from Stoke Edith station to destinations beyond Worcester.

Ledbury Junction station, looking towards Hereford from the ground above the tunnel, c. 1905. The train of four- or six-wheeled carriages hauled by a GWR saddle-tank locomotive in the foreground is signalled for the Gloucester branch, which curves away to the left beyond the station. The train is leaving its stabling point, the 'Gloucester' siding, and joining the main line. Behind the smoke of an incoming train from Hereford is Ledbury Viaduct. The goods shed dates from 1894. To the right of the station platform are sidings and cattle pens, which the inhabitants of Ledbury and district requested in a letter to the GWR directors in December 1888.

Ledbury station, looking towards Hereford, c. 1932. From January 1915, the heavier GWR classes of locomotives, including 4–6–0s and 2–8–0s, were permitted to use the main line through Ledbury on the W&HR. There had been many complaints about delays occurring at the single-line tunnel bottlenecks at both Ledbury and Colwall. Wartime emergency conditions no doubt prompted this decision, which enabled heavier loads of traffic to be carried.

Ledbury Town Halt, looking towards Gloucester under Bye Street Bridge, *c.* 1932. The halt opened in 1928, with the small station office which can be glimpsed beyond the corrugated-iron shelter. The 'Daffodil line', as it became popularly known, had been singled before the halt was opened, so there was plenty of space available for the wide platform. From 1940 onwards a GWR diesel railcar or an autocoach hauled by a '14XX' class 0–4–2T was the usual motive power supplied for use on the line by Cheltenham sub-shed. The halt closed with the end of the passenger service in 1959.

Ledbury Junction station, 1921, looking towards Hereford and the double junction of the Gloucester branch which opened throughout on 27 July 1885. The route to Barrs Court opened without ceremony as a single line between Malvern Wells and Shelwick Junction on 15 September 1861.

'Hall' class 4–6–0 *Misterton Hall* arrives at Ledbury with a Cardiff–Birmingham train, 18 August 1957. By this time the Gloucester branch had been reduced to a Down line connection only, while the station roof had lost its ornate ironwork and the platform had had its awning extended. Two years after this, the Gloucester branch was closed to passenger traffic.

Ledbury station, looking towards Colwall and the tunnel, August 1969. The three-car stop sign for DMUs, modernized platform lighting and the fact that many of the sidings have been lifted are signs of the times. The goods yard had been closed since September 1965. The 1,323yd tunnel remained a single, narrow, poorly ventilated bore, suffocating for steam age footplatemen; one ex-driver recalls how a hose pipe was dangled below the footplate so that fresh air could be sucked through it while their freight train was banked up the gradient through the smoke-filled tunnel.

Ledbury, 28 July 1961. Ex-GWR 2–8–0T No. 5245 was the shunting engine allocated to Ledbury (sub-shed to Hereford) at this time. This locomotive was used as a banking engine through the tunnel, as well as a yard shunter. There was no shed building, only the cover shown in the photograph, with a maintenance pit provided between the running rails. At other times in the 1950s, either a '56XX' class 0–6–2T or a 2–8–2T was allocated for this duty, and they would couple bunker next to the brake van to minimize smoke drift.

Ledbury station forecourt, c. 1952. The local bus provided both a transport link and competition for the railways. The railways hit back with excursion trains to the seaside and to local and national events. Reduced or concessionary fares were another common strategy to compete with the opposition on the roads.

Forty years separate this and the previous scene of Ledbury forecourt, with a local bus waiting to pick up passengers in each case. In the background of this scene, *c.* 1912, a GWR loco with an extended smokebox faces Hereford. The bridge was renewed in 1896. At 4 a.m. on the Sunday morning when renewal work started, the engineer's train of twenty wagons and one workmen's coach was being shunted into sidings beyond the bridge when a coupling broke. The resulting runaway broke through a stopblock above the road, and several wagons crashed into the road beyond this bridge. Fortunately for the workmen, their coach came to a halt in the siding.

Ledbury Viaduct under construction, *c.* 1860. Sir Morton Peto and Stephen Ballard (whose home was at Colwall) were the joint contractors for the works. An estimated 5,000,000 bricks were used in its construction, and the bricks for the thirty-one arches were made on site. (Ballard Collection, Hereford CRO)

Colwall station, looking towards the second tunnel entrance, *c.* 1955. The first tunnel proved very troublesome to excavate. In 1856, a Captain Penrice tried a patent steam tunnelling machine which only filled the bore with smoke. Tunnelling was a specialized occupation, labour was often short, and a band of hard, igneous rock was encountered, which meant it did not open for traffic until September 1861. In 1908, the union ASLEF took up complaints from Midland Railway goods train footplatemen about dangerously poor ventilation in the bore; one fireman had collapsed from the effects at one stage. The GWR eventually acted to improve matters, but decided that a new tunnel was the only solution. This single-line second bore opened in 1926, but plans to use both tunnels were abandoned, although the first tunnel was used to store ammunition during the Second World War.

A BR(W) 2–6–2T hauls its train up the adverse gradient from the tunnel into Colwall station, *c.* 1960. Many trains in this direction needed a banking engine to assist them up the 1 in 90 gradient, adding more smoke to an already poorly ventilated bore. The tunnel presented a bottleneck to traffic, although siding accommodation had been much increased in 1913 to provide more refuge space. The signal-box replaced an older one in 1927, and closed on 1 October 1967 when the line was singled.

The labourers of contractors Ballard and Brassey at work on Colwall Tunnel, c. 1860. A horse drags out some spoil in a wagon while several men are digging out drainage channels on the slopes of the cutting. (Hereford CRO)

BR-built 'Modified Hall' class 4–6–0 No. 6992 *Arborfield Hall* works hard against the 1-in-80 gradient at the east end of Ledbury Tunnel, c. 1953. The train, complete with headboard and chocolate and cream coloured coaches, is the 'Cathedrals' Express'. This was the Blue Riband service between Hereford and Paddington from the mid-1950s until dieselization in the mid-1960s. (Vickers)

# CHAPTER THREE

# THE GOLDEN VALLEY RAILWAY

*Pontypool Road GWR shed provided and serviced the locomotives that worked the mixed trains over the Golden Valley Railway route, with the engine housed in the small wooden shed at Pontrilas. From 1901 until 1933 the '517' class 0–4–2Ts, such as No. 1469 pictured here in 1924, were chosen as suitable for these duties. A mixed train has arrived from Hay, and stands in the bay platform at Pontrilas station. Fireman Cyril Davies stands on the footplate below the large brake dome, which has been painted over at some stage. Engineman Charlie Smith leans on the engine's coal bunker. Beyond Charlie is Guard Bert Jennings, with Station Master Bob Thurtle to the right.*

By the 1870s, Hay was a thriving market town on the River Wye, and Pontrilas was also a busy place at the southern end of the Dore Valley. Both towns had a railway connected to them, so some optimistic Victorians sought to link the two towns along the wide and relatively flat Dore or 'Golden' Valley. The plan of 1875 was not the first and neither had Hay always been regarded as the northern terminus, but the Golden Valley Railway ultimately connected the Hereford, Hay & Brecon line station at Hay with the Newport, Abergavenny & Hereford Railway route via a junction at Pontrilas.

Parliamentary proceedings pursuant to an Act took until 13 July 1876, but it was not until 1 September 1881 that the first 10 mile 56 chain section opened from Pontrilas to Dorstone. Problems with contractors, the bad winter weather and escalating costs all contributed to the slow progress.

However, a line only as far as Dorstone made little economic sense, and the extension of the railway to Hay was vigorously pursued. The prospectus of the time illustrated the line as part of a grand trunk route between Bristol and Liverpool.

The line linking Dorstone to Hay was eventually opened on 21 April 1889, and following engineering and land ownership difficulties over a direct entry to Hay, had to settle for a semi-circular route which entered the Wye Valley near Clifford, alongside what had become the Midland Railway's track from Hereford.

The GVR was a locally raised railway, but was inadequately financed from the beginning, and given its environs, was unlikely to generate profitable traffic returns. However, never short on optimism, not only the Hay extension but even a link to Monmouth were considered by some directors as ways to create a viable future for the company. At the same time, other factions were desperately trying to sell their railway to the GWR. This friction over the best means of achieving a financial return led to wholesale changes in the GVR's directorship before those who favoured independence had their way.

In the event, the Hay link did not produce any dramatic increase in traffic, but by the early 1890s, the decrease in income was at least slowed by some pioneer marketing of the area for leisure purposes. The independent GVR struggled on until 1897, once described as an 'eccentric railway', but more seriously, at other times, as unsafe for public use. At this stage the GWR saw that the run-down Golden Valley Railway could be bought at a bargain price and was worthy of their consideration. Entirely on their own terms, the GWR secured an Act of Parliament which vested them with the Golden Valley Railway from 1 July 1899.

On 1 May 1901, the GWR reopened the refurbished Golden Valley line using the same timetable as its predecessors – three mixed trains daily each way, a Wednesday (Hereford market day) special to Pontrilas from Dorstone, and a daily goods run to Hay and back when required. The excursion train made its appearance in the late 1920s, further expanding the horizons of the local population.

The 1930s saw more modern rolling stock in use, and locomotive power switched to the new '48XX' class 0–4–2Ts, but with declining numbers of passengers, the future was looking grim as road transport became a more viable alternative.

The Second World War and the choice in 1940 by HM Office of Works of Elm Bridge, between Pontrilas and Abbeydore stations, as the site for a private siding leading into an Ordnance depot gave a thirty-year boost to the longevity of the southern end of the Golden Valley line. However, the priority given to the Ordnance traffic finally curtailed what remained of the passenger timetable, and this officially ceased on 15 December 1941.

After the war, freight traffic along the whole branch kept going reasonably well until a decision was announced in 1949 that the line north of Dorstone would close from 1 January 1950. The remainder, south to Abbeydore, closed in piecemeal fashion, and only the last 1½ miles to Elm Bridge remained open until 1969, in order to provide rail access to the Ordnance depot.

GWR '517' class 0–4–2T No. 1437 waiting to start its train away to Hay from the Golden Valley line bay at Pontrilas station, 1909. In the background is the end of Pontrilas goods shed. The water crane alongside the locomotive dates from the time when the LNWR were responsible for the infrastructure of the line.

A '517' class 0–4–2T has arrived at Pontrilas station with a Golden Valley mixed train, *c.* 1910. The view is towards Hereford. The line to Hay-on-Wye leaves the main line to the left, and on the right are sidings leading to a small brickyard and tar distillation depot.

Crossing Keeper Mrs Watkins at Succours Lane crossing near Clifford, *c.* 1937. Each crossing on the Golden Valley Railway route had the gates padlocked against the railway, and each crossing had a keeper living in a lodge nearby, who was available to open the gates for the trains. Mrs Watkins operated the gates at Succours Lane from 1912 until closure in January 1950. Her husband was employed as a GWR ganger until 1932.

A GWR '517' class 0–4–2T runs into Peterchurch station with a mixed train from Pontrilas, *c.* 1908. This was generally considered to be the busiest of the stations in the Golden Valley. Landowners around Peterchurch village, such as the Robinson family, were the main supporters of the original Golden Valley Railway scheme, led by the proprietor of Peterchurch's large village stores, Mr C.E. Lane. Later, a group based around Hay joined in, and also canvassed for the promotion of the railway.

Passenger Guard Tidmas and Engineman Charlie Smith pose for the camera at Dorstone with a young visitor who has been invited on to the footplate of GWR '58XX' class 0–4–2T No. 5818 of Pontrilas shed, 1937. Looking towards Pontrilas, a second line of rails can be seen to the left, where there was once a second platform. Dorstone was the original terminus of the independent Golden Valley Railway when it opened on 1 September 1881. It became a terminus again when the line was truncated in December 1940. To the right of the picture is a small goods yard with a weighbridge facility.

'517' class 0–4–2T No. 1437 takes water at Pontrilas engine shed, 1909. Pontrilas was an outstation of Pontypool Road shed, which provided and serviced the branch locomotives. The first shed was also wooden, and burnt down, being replaced by the one in the photo. A large pump provided the power to extract water from a well to supply the tank.

Ex-Llanelly & Mynydd Mawr Railway 0–6–0ST No. 359 *Hilda*, standing alongside the running line outside Pontrilas shed, 1941. The engine and crew were on loan to Messrs Gee, Slater and Walker while construction of the Ordnance depot at Elm Bridge near Pontrilas took place. Notice the light dimensions of the original rails used in this siding.

Near Bacton crossing, 1941. Bacton station and siding were opened by the GWR in late 1901, following the reopening of the Golden Valley line. In 1941, this site was an unlikely choice for the delivery from the USA of Allis-Chalmers tractor components packed in crates, to be assembled on the spot. Here, looking towards Vowchurch, a '58XX' class 0–4–2T shunts open wagons, four of which contain finished tractors.

A GWR '517' class 0–4–2T travelling up to Hay bunker-first on a mixed train at Vowchurch, *c.* 1910. An outside-framed brake van brings up the rear. There was enough traffic at the time to warrant the employment of a station porter as well as Stationmaster Pinnock, who is pictured here on the right.

Vowchurch station, *c.* 1910. The stationmaster stands in front of the typical station buildings that were manufactured by the Gloucester Wagon Company to a design using tongued and grooved wood originating from Messrs Eassie and Co. The roof was tiled with slate and had ornate capping, finials and bargeboards. Inside was a heated waiting room, railway office and lamp room, along with toilets.

There was much activity between Pontrilas and Elm Bridge during 1940 and 1941, when this photograph was taken. Materials needed to strengthen the route up to the Ministry of Supply depot in order to allow heavier traffic to use it are being off-loaded from a Macaw 'B' wagon which has been hauled from Pontrilas by a '58XX' class 0–4–2T loco.

Advantage is being taken of Sunday closure of the line to load a large quantity of cord wood, probably for use as pit-props, near Vowchurch, 1927. Clearly, a large gang of loaders was needed for this task. The company initials LNWR can just be made out on the second wagon from the right, although it is five years since that company became part of the LMS.

Peterchurch station staff on the platform, *c.* 1930. The stationmaster is Ernest Sutton, who was promoted from signalman in South Wales to stationmaster at Peterchurch in about 1917. Mr Sutton retired from his post in 1944, by which time he was overseeing other stations along the line in addition to Peterchurch.

The Rector of Dorstone, the Revd George Powell (centre), attended the arrival of the last train to Dorstone, 30 January 1953. Mr Powell had links with the origins of the original Golden Valley Railway, being a son of the Revd T.P. Powell, a landowner and driving force behind the original company. Standing to the left of Mr Powell is Councillor A.E. Farr, Mayor of Hereford, who invited ex-Golden Valley Railway staff and their families to a farewell dinner in Hereford.

Small crossings, such as this, pictured in 1909, abounded on the Golden Valley route. This one is near the engine shed at Pontrilas, and looks back to the main line station. The chimney of the tar distillation plant can be seen in the background.

Abbeydore (the railway did not split the name into two) station, looking towards Pontrilas, *c.* 1930. A small siding was provided here, with a cattle pen. A stationmaster's house was built behind the station platform to the right of the road crossing.

# CHAPTER FOUR

# THE SHREWSBURY & HEREFORD RAILWAY

*North of Barrs Court, c. 1910. The LNWR goods shed is on the upper left, and was connected to the equivalent GWR shed by a footbridge across the running lines. This is seen below the high signal gantry positioned by the LNWR, which was responsible for signalling the Joint Line at this period. The arrangement of wagons in the goods sidings differed according to their load. The coal line is in the foreground, and the cattle wagons show evidence of the copious use of limewash as a disinfectant. Unloading activity is in full swing; hop-poles are about to be roped down on a flat cart, while a load of lime is being carted away to the right of the cattle vans. Open wagons predominate, many using sheeted covering to protect a bulky load of hay, for instance. Beyond the cattle pens to the right, round timber is stacked in quantity. In later years, after many other sidings in the station area were removed, this area became the preserve of the Engineering Department. (E. Jones Collection)*

In 1846, parliament opted for a 4 ft 8 in gauge line between Shrewsbury and Hereford when Henry Robertson's plan was sanctioned in preference to Brunel's broad gauge railway proposal. It took four years to manoeuvre the finances into such a position that a contractor, Thomas Brassey, felt able not only to build the line, but to have enough confidence in its prospects to offer to work the line at his own risk.

A single line was completed in stages, the final section being that to Hereford. It opened to goods on 30 July 1852, and to all traffic on 6 December 1853.

The LNWR, as ever looking for a route into South Wales and already enjoying running powers to Hereford over the S&HR, diplomatically proposed a joint lease with the GWR, but with the sub-text of extending their running powers to their own advantage. The GWR would not be tempted at first, but after much in-fighting the S&HR became the joint property of the LNWR, GWR and the West Midland Railway on 1 July 1862. Arrangements were then made to double the line south of Ludlow, with the exception of Dinmore tunnel.

The WMR, having amalgamated with the GWR, passed on their interests in the S&HR, and under an Act of 1871, the LNWR and GWR jointly acquired the S&HR.

In 1887, the traffic levels were boosted by the opening of the Severn Tunnel, and Hereford became the first stop after Bristol on the west–north expresses. From May 1892, the conversion to standard gauge of the previously broad gauge lines west of Exeter meant even longer-distance through services, calling at Barrs Court station.

After playing a major role in the distribution of steam coal during the First World War, 1922 found the route in the hands of the GWR/LMS Joint Company. This continued until 1948, when nationalization placed the Herefordshire section of the line in the Western Region of British Railways. The end of steam traction and the closure of uneconomical branches throughout the Marches in the early 1960s set the railway outlook to 'unsettled'. Thoughts surfaced of diverting all traffic from the south via Birmingham through Shelwick Junction.

By 1972, the daily passenger service had been cut back, and only ran between Cardiff and Shrewsbury or Crewe, longer-distance passenger trains being confined to summer Saturdays only. Sectorization in 1984 brought a reversal of fortunes for Barrs Court and the ex-S&HR line with an extension of their services, notably to Manchester, a policy which, with improved rolling stock and facilities, continued the upward trend of passenger returns into the early 1990s.

In the summer of 1997, the true 'North & West' nature of Hereford's railway past returned with Penzance–Manchester trains being announced on the Barrs Court public address system.

At privatization, Prism Rail won the franchise for the South West & Wales Railway, which had dropped the word 'South' from its title by 1998.

Throughout the doldrum years for passenger traffic, freight traffic managed to keep the line going, but even this began to disappear in the early 1990s. However, since Transrail's 'Enterprise' service, a return to wagonload traffic in 1994, the decline has halted and finally reversed under the initiative of the English, Welsh & Scottish railway freight traffic policy since 1997.

Naturally, a huge variety of locomotives, steam and diesel, would have visited Barrs Court on 'North & West' line trains. The first through trains between Bristol and Shrewsbury were hauled by 2–4–0 locomotives, culminating in the GWR '3232' class as passenger trains became heavier. GWR 'Badminton' class 4–4–0s became associated with main line duties through Hereford at the turn of the century, as did the GWR 'County' class 4–4–0s and later still the 'Saint' class 4–6–0s, or 'Hereford Castles' as they became nicknamed.

The line was truly joint, however, and LNWR types played their part on local trains as they did on heavy goods workings.

A brief extract from an enthusiast's record of 'North & West' route train observations at Barrs Court station on 20 December 1927 should give a taste of the past (in some cases, the engines are still numbered as in LNWR days):

GWR locos on passenger trains 'Saint' class: 2903/5/24/32/36/48/50.
'County' 4–4–0 class: 3801/24.
'Bulldog' class: 3303/17/49/80/3/95.
LMS locos – 'George the Fifth' class: 1532.
'Prince of Wales' class: 1196/2392/5606, and on goods: 285/2108/2369/3359/8849.

Ex-GWR 'Castle' class 4–6–0 No. 5081 *Lockheed Hudson* backs on to a waiting train at Ayleston (the GWR preferred this spelling) Hill signal-box, 20 June 1956. The carriage sidings can be seen in the background, once the site of the broad gauge engine shed. The name of the locomotive was altered from *Penrice Castle* in January 1941, to recognize the role of the aircraft in the Battle of Britain.

Station staff outside the entrance to Leominster station on the occasion of the visit to the town of HM Queen Elizabeth II.

A typical scene at Barrs Court station, late 1950s. The carriage stock on view is all in maroon livery, and ex-GWR 'Castle' class 4–6–0 No. 5043 *Earl of Mount Edgecumbe* has worked through from Paddington on a train that in earlier years would have changed engines at Worcester (Shrub Hill). The locomotive represents the 'Castle' class in its final form, with double chimney (altered October 1956) and Hawksworth flat-sided tender. No. 5043 was withdrawn in December 1963.

A Canton ex-GWR 'Castle' class 4–6–0, one of the 50XX 'Earl' series, sweeps into Barrs Court under the Aylestone Hill roadbridge, 30 May 1952. Cardiff Canton shed (86C) cleaning staff had a reputation in the 1950s for sending out their own 'Castle' class locomotives in good order. To the right, the sidings contain two ex-GWR 'Cordon' tank wagons, whose function was to supply gas for lighting carriage stock of the older design, seen also in the siding and in Engineering or Signal Department use at this time. The old broad gauge engine shed on the left is still in use for stabling carriages. (E. Morton)

An ex-GWR '51XX' Class 2–6–2T No. 4141 at the south end of Barrs Court, on empty carriage stock duty, June 1951. An elegant ex-GWR Hawksworth-designed carriage is seen coupled to the locomotive.

BR '03' class 0–6–0 diesel mechanical shunter No. D2132 pauses at the north end of Barrs Court station, 1966. The 'wasp' warning markings of yellow-and-black chevrons on the cab were part of an overall trend towards a safer working environment for railway workers during this era.

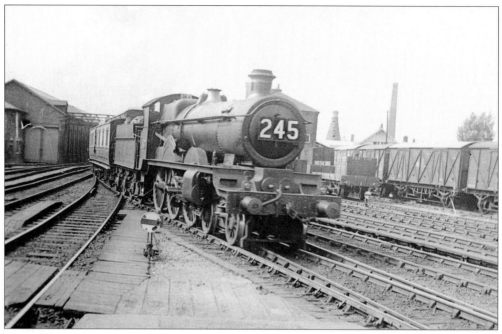

A 'Saint' class 4–6–0 runs into Barrs Court from the north, *c.* 1930. The reporting number '245' carried on the smokebox indicates that it is a Liverpool–Plymouth Saturdays-only train. The long vans in the sidings to the right most likely contained consignments of perishables, probably fruit.

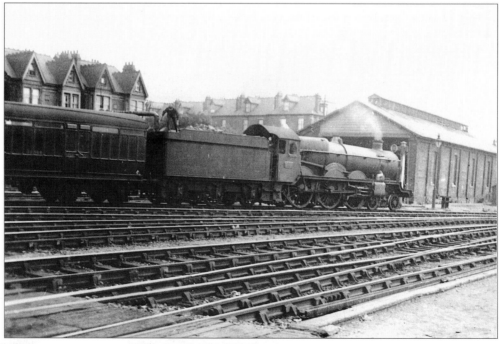

Tall houses in Barrs Court Road and Aylestone Hill overlook a fireman as he deals with the 'bag' to supply water to the tender of a GWR 4–6–0 as it prepares to head south-west. The ex-broad gauge engine shed is behind the locomotive. An ex-LNWR full brake carriage is coupled up to the engine.

Re-laying of the Down relief line track with concrete sleepers in progress in 1973 outside the signal-box which was renamed 'Hereford station signal-box' in June of that year. Earlier LNWR signals had been replaced by standard ex-GWR types by this time. (A. Vaughan)

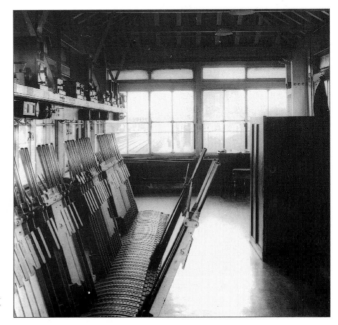

Inside Hereford station signal-box, looking south, 1973. (A. Vaughan)

Clerestory coaches at Barrs Court station, *c.* 1910. The coach in the bay to the right will form part of a Midland Railway train on the Hay & Brecon route.

Barrs Court station, *c.* 1956. The un-rebuilt and unnamed ex-LMS 'Patriot' class 4–6–0 No. 45551 prepares to head north. The ex-LNWR goods shed is to the right.

The demolition of the ex-LNWR goods shed at Barrs Court station, November 1986.

'Castle' class 4–6–0 No. 7007 *Great Western* at Barrs Court station. The name and company coat of arms on the wheel splasher commemorate the fact that it was the last of its class to be built at Swindon works (1946) under GWR ownership. It was not given a double chimney until 1961, and was then withdrawn in February 1963. The Shrewsbury service was already being run by a DMU; No. 7007 was at work on Worcester route stopping trains at the time. (Andrew Ingram)

A view from Aylestone Hill overbridge in 1962, when steam and diesel traction existed side by side at Barrs Court station. A 'Hymek' has just arrived on a Paddington express, a 'Warship' class pauses on a parcels train, while Stanier 8F 2–8–0 No. 48326 has right of way towards Abergavenny.

Ex-LMS 'Royal Scot' class 4–6–0 No. 46129 *The Scottish Horse* rolls its train past College Road sidings to the right and past the site of the LNWR loco shed, 1962. To the left is the Brecon Curve with the Brecon Curve signal-box. In the background are Messrs Painter Bros Ltd's construction towers and the gasometer store of Hereford gasworks. (A. Vickers)

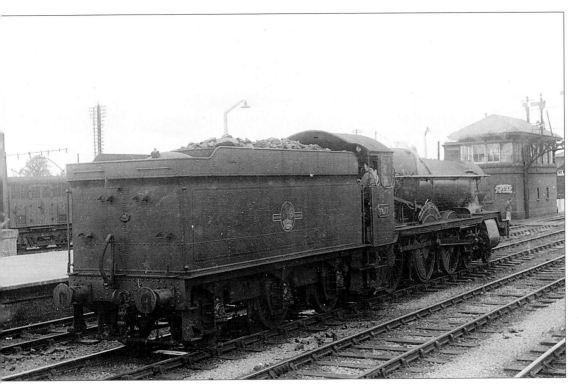

Ex-GWR 'Grange' class 4–6–0 No. 6877 *Llanfair Grange* sits quietly on the Down relief line, 1957. Beyond the station signal-box is the ex-GWR goods shed.

GWR '517' class 0–4–2T No. 1421 at Barrs Court, facing south by the footbridge, 1927. There appear to be plenty of customers joining the GWR clerestory coaches on the platform alongside.

Ex-LMS 'Jubilee' class 4–6–0 No. 45699 *Galatea* of Shrewsbury shed eases its train out of the southern end of Dinmore tunnel, spring 1963. The viewpoint is close by the Railway Inn, whose premises had served for the inquest into the death of a navvy, Thomas Mills, crushed in 1893 by a fall of rocks during blasting in the second tunnel. (A. Vickers)

Ex-GWR 'Hall' class 4–6–0 No. 4916 *Crumlin Hall* works past the old station building below the skew bridge at Dinmore, 1963. The skew was put into the bridge when it was realigned to squeeze in a waiting room on the new Up platform of 1893, when the second tunnel came into use. The Up line is raised in relation to the Down as a result of the second tunnel bore.

Dinmore station, looking north, *c.* 1910. Against the contractor Thomas Brassey's advice, the 1,060 yd long tunnel was built to be suitable for a single line only, unlike the remainder of the S&HR route. For the ceremonial opening on 6 September 1853, the last of approximately 3,250,000 bricks had been gilded, and was laid by Mrs Field, wife of the General Superintendent of Works. The left-hand bore was added in 1893, when traffic had increased, partly as a result of the opening of the Severn Tunnel in 1888 and the extension beyond Exeter of the GWR's 4 ft 8 in gauge.

Hereford, looking north towards the Brecon Curve, 1920s. The three-bay ex-LNWR engine shed is on the right, with an ex-LNWR locomotive in view. Hereford shed was allocated the number 31 by the LNWR in 1857, but by the date of this photograph it had been demoted to become a sub-shed under the supervision of Abergavenny LMS shed. Facilities were minimal; coaling was done by hand from wagons drawn up into the shed, but a turntable existed beyond the bracket signals above the locomotive. The sidings on the left linked to the GWR goods shed.

Two of the many privately owned wagons with outlets in Hereford's sidings in the last quarter of the nineteenth century and until the Second World War. They were used mainly for coal, coke and other minerals at first, and later tanks carrying fuel were introduced. As a bonus, the wagons acted as mobile advertisements for their owners. Other owners in Hereford included Nash and Company and Edwin Munslow. (HMRS)

Motorized public transport in the form of an open-top omnibus pulling away from Barrs Court station, December 1913. Horse-drawn vehicles and hand carts still predominate. The tall chimney-stacks of the station reveal a Gothic influence in the design of the station. One of these stacks was to come crashing to the ground in an earth tremor which affected the district in May 1925.

The concourse of Barrs Court station, *c.* 1910. At the time, R.T. Smith & Co. of Gloucester were the GWR's main parcels agent in the area. The refreshment room to the left of the entrance advertises Bass beer, while White Star liners have a poster displayed. The station clock is set into the wall at this period, and one of the group of three men includes a top hat in his uniform.

By 1979 Barrs Court station concourse had lost the canopy over the main entrance, but had gained one over the parcel depot entrance.

Barrs Court station, looking north, August 1969, when the fabric of the station was in a very run-down state. The track layout had been rationalized the year before. Many crossings were lifted, and the Down relief was taken out altogether, but was replaced in 1973.

Barrs Court station, looking south, late 1920s. A GWR 4–4–0 stands with some parcels vehicles, while the LMS train to Brecon awaits passengers in the bay to the right. One of the scissors crossings which once linked the platform roads to the through lines on both Up and Down routes is just visible halfway down the north-bound platform.

Ex-GWR 'Churchward Mogul' 2–6–0 No. 4358 in fully lined green livery waiting alongside the Barrs Court station signal-box with a train from the Ross & Gloucester line, 26 May 1957. (N.L. Browne via F. Hornby)

Looking down from Aylestone Hill overbridge into Barrs Court station, late 1920s. The area where several horseboxes, a milk van and a gas cylinder wagon are standing had been a covered carriage shed until 1916. A clerestory coach rests outside the shed, which was then in use for carriages. Outside the station entrance a taxi rank is just visible.

A quiet spell at Barrs Court station, looking south, *c.* 1910. An MR carriage stands in the Brecon line bay on the right-hand side.

LMS Fowler 2–6–4T No. 2354 stands at the south end of Barrs Court station, no doubt awaiting duty to take a train on in the Abergavenny direction, *c.* 1935. (HMRS)

The first member of the Beames Ex-LNWR 0–8–4Ts, No. 7930, rated at 7F power classification by the LMS, taking water and about to continue its journey towards Abergavenny, *c.* 1930. Behind the loco is Commercial Road, with much competitive road traffic and two large car showrooms in evidence. (HMRS)

Barrs Court Junction, previously Barton Junction, *c.* 1929. The signal-box replaced another in 1878, and closed in July 1966. The lines bringing traffic to and from Shelwick Junction on the left veer into Barrs Court station, while straight ahead the so-called 'Worcester mile', the avoiding line through Moorfields and Barton, can be viewed below the right belonging to Messrs Painter Bros and looking towards Watkin's Flour Mill. As a result of the extra traffic demand brought on by the war, the junction was altered in 1941 to add an Up and Down goods track through Barrs Court station. The route to Barton was then severed in 1967, leaving a short stub to provide a private siding to H. Wiggins & Co. Ltd as the firm was then known.

Barton and Brecon Curve Junction, *c.* 1930, showing the signal-box which was closed in 1937. To the right are the line from Barrs Court and the Brecon Curve, opened on 1 January 1893 and singled in 1967. Beyond the junction lies a gated private siding to Groom's woodyard. To the left, the line of coal wagons stand on a siding leading to the City of Hereford Gasworks and a siding off connects with Painter Bros, while the middle siding with the high-sided coke wagon is part of the Show Yard sidings.

BR 'Britannia' class 7MT 4–6–2 No. 70023 *Venus* of Cardiff Canton shed waits by Barrs Court station signal-box on a train from its home town, July 1958.

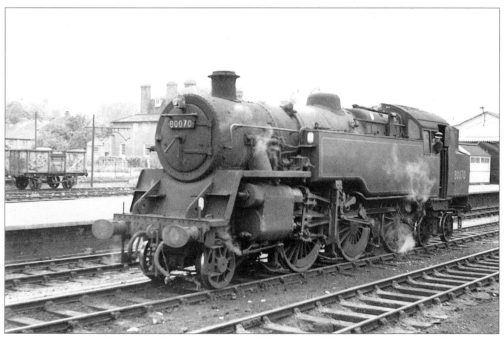

BR 'Standard' class 4MT 2–6–4T No. 80070 of Shrewsbury shed stands at the north end of Barrs Court station, July 1963. The engine displays 'Danger. Overhead Electrical Wires' warning notices above the bufferbeam and on the front of the tank.

BR 'Standard' class 4MT 4–6–0 No. 75029 arrives at Barrs Court, July 1957. It has been fitted with a double chimney and is in BR green livery with orange-and-black lining.

BR 'Standard' class 5MT 4–6–0 No. 73132 awaits departure time at the southern end of Barrs Court station, July 1957. The back wall of the carriage shed that was converted from the original engine shed still stands. By this date, Hereford shed had been allocated its own BR 'Standard' class locomotive, 2–6–0 2MT No. 78004. This locomotive's main duty was working the Brecon line trains from Barrs Court.

38XX 'County' class 4–4–0 No. 3817 *County of Monmouth* at the north end of Barrs Court station, *c.* 1910. This locomotive was built in 1906, and was one of the class which had its original cast-iron chimney replaced by a larger copper-topped version from 1907. G.J. Churchward is reputed to have produced this class in response to the LNWR's refusal to allow a 'Saint' class 4–6–0 over the Hereford–Shrewsbury route. Locomotives of this class were some of the first to appear liveried with the GWR garter crest on the tender.

This is '806' class 2–4–0 No. 819 at Barrs Court station. The carriage stock in the background behind the close-up footplate view appears to be MR in design, but offers no clue from its livery to date the photograph. However, No. 819 was condemned for scrap in September 1913.

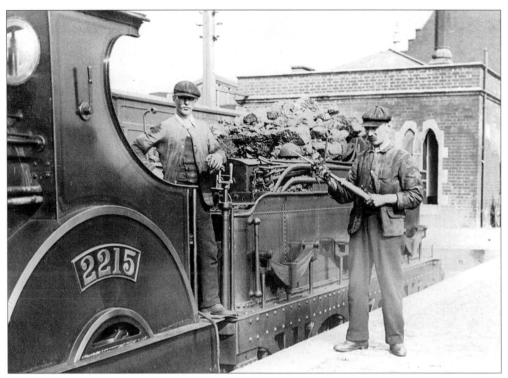

A GWR '2201' class 2–4–0, a William Dean development of Armstrong's '806' class, in the north end bay at Barrs Court station. The well-polished arched number-plate and brass beading on the splasher of the 6 ft 7 in coupled wheel are noteworthy on this locomotive, which was condemned in January 1909.

GWR 38XX 'County' class 4–4–0 No. 3818 *County of Radnor* stands in Barrs Court station facing north, some time between December 1906 (when it was built) and October 1910 (when a superheater was added). Both scissor crossover formations at mid-platform length show well on this photograph. The station bookstall is apparent, too.

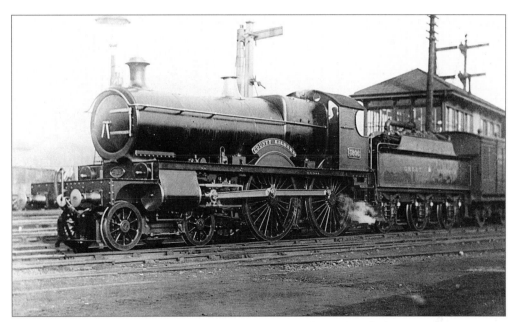

GWR 38XX 'County' class 4–4–0 No. 3806 *County Kildare* at the north end of Barrs Court station soon after being released for traffic in 1906. The original 'pinched' style of cast-iron chimney is apparent. The first ten names of this Churchward design celebrated the growing GWR connection with Ireland via Fishguard. The LNWR ventilated van behind the locomotive was built to carry perishable goods coupled to express passenger trains. No. 3806 is probably waiting to add this load to a Shrewsbury-bound train and take over as train engine.

GWR 'Flower' class 4–4–0 No. 4112 *Carnation* faces north at Barrs Court station, *c.* 1909. William Dean developed this class, with its 6 ft 8 in coupled driving wheels, from the similar re-boilered 'Atbara' class 4–4–0s. They were part of the company's strategy to replace 4–2–2 and 2–4–0 engines on GWR express services.

Dean 'Flower' class 4–4–0 No. 4105 *Camellia* at the north end of Barrs Court station, *c.* 1909.

An unidentified GWR 38XX 'County' class 4–4–0 drifts into Barrs Court with an express from the north, passing under the footbridge that connected the GWR and LNWR goods sheds. The locomotive is not superheated, and neither does it have top feed, which dates the photograph between 1904 and 1909. The works plate is visible below the smokebox door on these engines, which were among the first GWR types to have black frames and cylinders, replacing Indian red.

Ford Bridge station, looking towards Hereford and the level-crossing, *c.* 1920, when new accommodation was being constructed. The platform either side of the running line had been extended by 1890, by which time a siding and crossover had been added to the original simple through lines.

LMS 'Prince of Wales' class 4–6–0 No. 5632 *Bret Harte* of shed 30 stands facing north in Barrs Court station, 7 August 1932. No. 5632 was one of five members of the class to be rebuilt during 1923–24, being fitted with outside Walschaerts valve gear.

BR 'Standard' Class 7MT 4–6–2 No. 70025 *Western Star* heads south past Pinsley Flourmill and Bromyard Junction at the north end of Leominster station, April 1961. The junction and crossover were removed later that year. The engine shed, just visible through the smoke, closed a year after this view was taken.

Ex-WD 2–8–0 No. 90563 hurries a Down freight at the northern end of Leominster station, September 1951. To the right is the brick base, all that remains of the Bromyard Junction signal-box, closed in 1901, then converted to a shed for other uses. (J. Edgington)

LNWR-type signals dominate this view south from Leominster station, *c.* 1920, which shows the layout of lines dating from changes made during 1901–2. The original engine shed stood to the left of the platform, slightly nearer to the station than the goods shed. The economic sense of using a horse to shunt a wagon is demonstrated outside the goods shed to the right of the picture.

Staff at Leominster station predominate in the crowds posing for the camera. The continuation of the footbridge to the right out of the picture suggests that the Steens Bridge line and the platform is ready (1 March 1887) or in use. The shunting horse stands on the permanent way, ballasted to completely cover the sleepers, as was the mode at this period. The elevated signal-box of 1901 has yet to be built.

The South End signal-box at Leominster, 1994. Opened in 1875, the design is typical of the hip-roofed style adopted by the Joint LNWR/GWR Company.

Leominster station, looking south, *c.* 1910. The signal-box was opened in 1902, and was elevated to save space on the platform. It closed in 1964. The carriages to the left are at the platform reserved for services to one of the three branches from Leominster: Kington, Bromyard and Tenbury.

The guard holds a conversation with the driver of the Kington branch train which has just arrived at the south end of Leominster station, 1951. The train is hauling a two-coach 'B' set. In the far distance an ex-LNWR 0–8–0 waits to proceed with a goods train. (R.C. Riley)

An ex-GWR 'Castle' class 4–6–0 leans to the curve of the super-elevated track just north of Leominster station. The engine shed is partly obscured to the right.

Another turn-of-the-century view at Leominster, looking south.

The two-road through shed at Leominster, sub-shed to Hereford 85C, contains ex-GWR '74XX' class 0–6–0PT No. 7426, employed as yard shunter or on branch freight working, *c.* 1955. The shed replaced an earlier one sited at the southern end of the station in 1901, and was closed on 30 April 1962. The open wagons to the right stand on the position of a turntable.

Berrington and Eye station, looking towards Leominster, *c.* 1930. The sidings contain privately owned coal wagons, including one belonging to Blake of Hereford. A temporary platform was moved south prior to the opening of the second line in 1864.

The signal-box at Berrington and Eye station was replaced by a groundframe in 1957, when only one entrance to the sidings, furthest from the station, was available. This situation is apparent as ex-GWR 10XX 'County' class 4–6–0 No. 1003 *County of Wilts* from Shrewsbury shed (84G) swings the 8.00 a.m. Plymouth–Liverpool express around the curve, 22 February 1958. All sidings had been taken out of use by the end of January 1961.

A light snow dusts the permanent way as ex-LMS '8F' class 2–8–0 thunders across Moreton-on-Lugg level-crossing with a goods train heading north past the signal-box, February 1958. Perhaps the two train spotters could identify the engine? The signal-box is a 1943 replacement box, coinciding with major developments in reception sidings and connections into a War Department Ordnance depot. These sidings and the rail entrance to the depot were on the far left, upper in the photograph.

Ex-LMS 'Stanier' Class 5 4–6–0 No. 44749 approaches the platform end at Leominster station, heading south, c. 1955. This locomotive was one of a batch in this class fitted with roller bearings and Caprotti valve gear. (J. Moss)

A mixed-traffic locomotive painted black is hauling a set of carmine-and-cream-painted carriages, a typical train of British Railways (Western Region) days. Hereford shed's own ex-GWR 49XX 'Hall' class 4–6–0 No. 6916 *Misterton Hall*, built in June 1941, is pictured with a stopping train from Worcester and Paddington on 30 May 1952. The clean-cut lines of a Hawksworth brake third carriage can be seen next to the engine, whose tender shows no sign of ownership nor, unlike the locomotive, any lining-out livery. The old wooden signal gantry has been replaced by one with tubular steel supports.

Ex-GWR 49XX 'Hall' class No. 6939 *Calveley Hall* of Cardiff Canton shed (86C) stands at Barrs Court in front of the ex-LNWR goods shed, 25 May 1957. This loco is attached to a Hawksworth straight-sided tender. (N. Browne)

GWR '481' class 2–4–0 No. 481 has arrived at Barrs Court, probably from Worcester, *c.* 1910. This locomotive was built in 1869, then 'renewed' at Swindon factory during 1888–89, taking on the appearance in the photograph. No. 481 was withdrawn in July 1912.

GWR 'Standard Goods' class 0–6–0 No. 411 shunts at the north end of Barrs Court station. A non-corridor GWR carriage is being added to a train already made up of non-passenger and non-GWR stock. The open wagon has a tall lamp attached, as if it is to be part of the train. It has what appear to be churns as its load. A Dean single-wheeled locomotive is just in view to the right. (HMRS)

# CHAPTER FIVE

# HEREFORD, HAY & BRECON
# RAILWAY

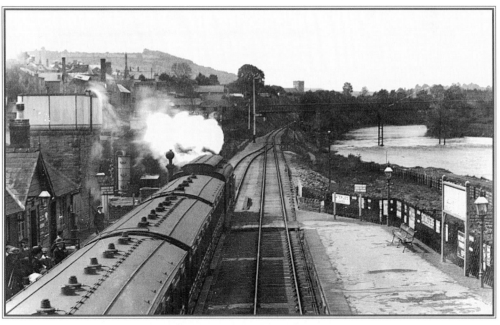

*The Midland Railway station alongside the River Wye at Hay, facing Brecon, c. 1910. In view is the wrought-iron bridge of 1865, which replaced, at a raised level, an earlier structure. The train's first vehicle is the through coach to Swansea from Birmingham, and the locomotive is likely to be a Johnson MR 0—4—4T taking on water, which these non-tender engines had to do at every opportunity on the journey.*

In 1845, the proposed Welsh Midland Railway attempted to purchase the horse-drawn Hay Railway with the intention of using its trackbed from Hereford to Brecon as part of a Birmingham–Swansea route. This failed, and it was thirteen years before a successful scheme for a Hereford–Brecon railway led to an Act of Parliament incorporating the Hereford, Hay & Brecon Railway on 1 August 1859.

The promoters of the Hereford, Hay & Brecon Railway sought local finance, but in reality they shared the greater ambition of the earlier scheme to provide a connecting link from the West Midlands to South Wales, and to Swansea and Fishguard in particular.

The early years of this company were characterized by many alterations in organization. Initially, the OWWR were to work the 38 mile line under an agreement including a share in the use of Barrs Court station. The rapid changes brought about by company amalgamations at the time overtook these proposals as, in turn, the NAHR and then the West Midland Railway inherited the OWWR's working agreement, and it was the latter which worked the initial Hereford–Eardisley section from a station at Moorfields, where very basic facilities had been made available for passenger trains from 30 June 1863.

By July 1864, when the line had been opened as far as Hay, the GWR had absorbed the WMR, and hired out locomotives to the Line's contractor, Thomas Savin, who took over responsibility for working the line until February 1866. Sharp, Stewart and Co. 2–4–0 locomotives were Savin's preferred motive power, and at least three of them were at work on Hereford & Brecon trains at this time.

Irregular arrangements continued to typify the HH&BR as it relocated its Hereford terminus to Barton in August 1864.

The next episode in the saga of the HH&BR's early years was amalgamation with the Brecon & Merthyr Railway, with which it shared the route to Brecon beyond Talyllyn Junction. When this amalgamation was discovered to be legally flawed, the HH&BR was placed in serious financial distress, and with Thomas Savin now bankrupt and the B&MR unable to continue working the traffic, the Mid Wales Railway stepped into the gap and kept the services going from 16 March 1868 until 30 September 1869, using Barton station.

During this period the Midland Railway had achieved access to Hereford with running powers over the Worcester & Hereford route. In 1869 the GWR successfully opposed the first attempt by the HH&BR to invite the MR to take it over, but a working agreement was nevertheless set up, with Moorfields reused as the terminus. At first the GWR had physically blocked the MR's path into Barton station, but a permanent lease of the HH&BR to the MR was agreed from 1 September 1874, with a further move back to Barton station. The station for Brecon line trains changed for a final time when the MR used a newly opened connection – the Brecon Curve – to reach Barrs Court.

Under MR management, traffic increased to include through coaches between Birmingham and Swansea, and overnight through goods trains along the same route. Johnson 0–6–0Ts and 0–4–4Ts worked the passenger trains, with Johnson 0–6–0 tender goods kept for the goods services.

Following the grouping, the LMS lost much of the line's goods traffic after 1932 as a result of a policy change in organization, but then the changed requirements of the Second World War reversed some of the losses, with RAF Credenhill playing a major role. The war marked the advent of the first of the ex-L&YR 0–6–0 tender engines that came to be closely associated with the line in late LMS days. Later, in the early 1950s, ex-LMS 3F 0–6–0s arrived, but proved too heavy, and their place was eventually taken by Ivatt 2–6–0 tender engines, which proved ideal for the passenger timetable.

The arrival of British Railways management soon rationalized the regional arrangement from LMR to Western Region from 2 April 1950, when ex-GWR types such as 'Dean Goods', 57XX 0–6–0PTs and 2251 0–6–0s ousted the LMR types. A DMU was tried out, but Moorhampton bank proved beyond its capacity and steam traction remained until the end. The passenger service finished on 31 December 1962, while a truncated goods operation existed, to Eardisley only, until September 1964.

Whitney-on-the-Wye, looking towards Hay and the River Wye bridge, *c*. 1910. Stationmaster at the time was Mr M. Morgan, who had transferred from Ystalyfera in 1894, and remained until retirement in 1924. The station opened under the name Whitney, had 'on-the-Wye' added in March 1880, and then became 'Whitney on Wye' in July 1924. A small siding with a cattle pen was operated by groundframe after the use of a signal-box ceased in 1892. The station became a temporary terminus for just over two weeks in December 1961, when the Wye Bridge was closed after flood damage.

Kinnersley station, looking towards Eardisley, *c*. 1912. The number two groundframe cabin, which replaced an earlier signal-box in about 1907, is just visible under the bridge, which was altered in 1901. The siding has a cattle pen and a sleeper-built platform to enable unloading of such items as barrels of beer, seen here awaiting collection, probably on arrival direct from the brewery at Burton for sale at the nearby Kinnersley Arms Hotel.

Ex-Van Railway, Manning, Wardle 0–6–0ST No. 25 was sold to HM Office of Works in June 1917, and was sent to work at Credenhill, where a rail-connected outpost of ROF Rotherwas had been established. Substantial sidings and loading facilities were established on the Hereford side of the station and a run-round goods loop, a replacement signal-box and an altered goods yard layout were in use by 1917.

Eardisley station Midland Railway staff, probably during the First World War, judging by the presence of Miss Parry on the station staff. Also pictured seated, left to right, are Stationmaster Parry (with dog), Senior Signalman Thomas Clerk and Ernest Brooks. Standing, left to right, are Bill Bevan, Mr Duggan of the Permanent Way Department, and Bill Thomas, Signalman. The South Wales–Birmingham via Worcester service, which ceased in 1916, is advertised on the poster behind the staff.

Eardisley station, looking towards Hay, *c.* 1917. The left-hand signal arm on the MR bracket signal has been removed, as this controlled the route of the GWR's line to Titley Junction. Eardisley Junction was closed from 1 January 1917, and the rails to Titley were lifted and shipped to Europe as part of the war effort. The track was subsequently relaid, and traffic was restored in December 1922.

A busy interlude at Eardisley, looking towards Hereford, *c.* 1890. The GWR branch passenger train has just arrived from the Titley branch direction, and its passengers cross the line on the level. A porter has a barrowful of parcels to wheel along the platform. In the distance the MR goods waits to continue its journey to Brecon, and is about to be crossed by an MR goods train in the opposite direction.

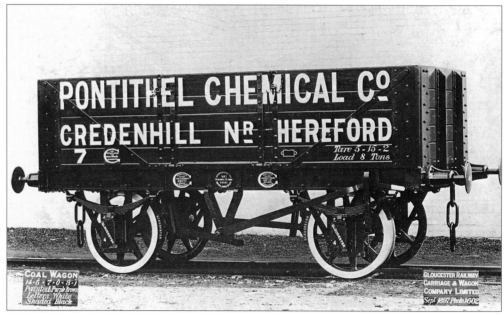

A wagon belonging to the Pontithel Chemical Co., which used a private siding at Mansell Lacy near Credenhill in addition to one at Pontithel itself. In 1873, the MR ordered a plan and estimated cost for the siding, and it remained in use until about 1928. The chemical works produced charcoal, wood naptha, acetate of lime and wood tar, all derived from waste timber. In addition, house coal and paraffin were sold locally. (HMRS)

A light fall of snow covers Moorfields yard, Hereford, looking towards the Brecon Curve and the ex-MR engine shed which closed on 12 December 1924, shortly before this view was taken. The timber-laden trailer on the left stands approximately on the site of the original Moorfields station platform, so the line in the foreground ran on into Barton station. Fuel to be transported in barrels is evident on the left, and a traction engine stands in the shadow of the timber pile. On the far right, rows of cattle trucks are concentrated in the GWR's Worcester sidings.

# CHAPTER SIX

# LEOMINSTER & KINGTON RAILWAY

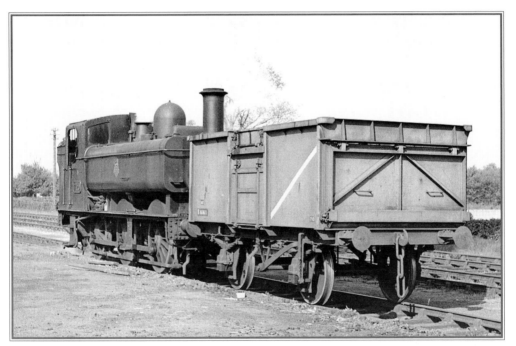

*'74XX' class 0–6–0PT No. 7420 shunts at Titley, 15 May 1956. At this stage several bridges on the line had become unsafe to be crossed by any loco heavier than the '74XX' class. Freight trains were restricted to haulage by one of three of the type that were then allocated to Leominster sub-shed. On 5 February 1955, No. 7420 and brake third coach W4345 had worked the last 'official' passenger train from Kington, the 4.55 p.m. to Leominster. The last train on the branch in the other direction was the 8.25 p.m. hauled by 0–4–2T No. 1413 with 70 ft auto trailer W67W. Normally, this would have returned as empty stock, but on this occasion, it ran with 55 passengers holding a wake, and left Kington at 9.11 p.m. (Hugh Davies)*

One of the great unfulfilled projects of the Victorian railway promoters was to build a line from Central England across mid-Wales to a port somewhere around Aberystwyth, to tap the lucrative Irish and Atlantic trades. Kington featured on most of these proposed routes of 1845–46, but when high hopes of becoming part of an important trunk route came to nothing, sights were set on a local West Herefordshire railway to link up with Leominster, where the Shrewsbury & Hereford Railway had planned a station.

Under the guidance of its leading promoter, Lord Bateman, an Act of 10 July 1854 incorporated the Leominster & Kington Railway Company. Progress with construction was very slow and the railway came into being in piecemeal fashion. The Leominster–Pembridge section opened for goods from 18 October 1855. With finances all but used up, a loan from contractors Brassey and Field was needed to complete the line to Kington. The formal opening of the 13 mile 25 chain line took place on 27 July 1857, but not without the need for another Act to overcome legal problems over a level-crossing at Pembridge.

By 1859 the contractors offered to buy out their contract, so dire were their returns. The directors would not agree, and instead unsuccessfully sought assistance from the neighbouring S&HR at the end of Brassey and Field's contract period.

The newly formed West Midland Railway, one of the joint lessees of the Shrewsbury–Newport line, came to the aid of the L&KR in a leasing deal from 1 July 1862. This arrangement was continued in slightly altered financial form by the successors to the WMR, the GWR. On 10 September 1875, the L&KR opened a 5½ mile branch to Presteign from Titley. The local company finally amalgamated with the GWR on 1 July 1898.

The Leominster–Kington branch passenger service closed for two months during the 1951 fuel crisis, and then reopened for four more years before closing to passengers on 5 February 1955. A skeleton freight service managed another nine years of service until 24 September 1964.

## The Kington & Eardisley Railway

When the Hay Tramway was sold to the Hereford, Hay & Brecon Railway Company in 1859 and the Kington Tramway was not incorporated into the Leominster & Kington Railway, contractor Thomas Savin persuaded local people to help finance a replacement standard gauge railway to maintain commercial contact between West Herefordshire and South Wales. This concern, the Kington & Eardisley Railway, received its Act on 30 June 1862, and followed broadly the direction of the Kington Tramroad south of Lyonshall. A branch from Lyonshall to the L&KR ½ mile west of Marston was also authorized. A second Act was obtained on 14 July 1864 for an extension to Presteigne (spelt Presteign by the railways – see page 99) that was never built, but running powers over the L&KR between Titley and Kington were granted. A detached section of the K&ER route from Kington to New Radnor was opened on 25 September 1875. As part of economies carried out during the First World War, the K&ER closed on 1 January 1917, and the junction was lifted. Restoration was effected on 11 December 1922, but lasted only until 1 July 1940, when the branch closed for good. The stub end at Eardisley remained in use, however, as an oil fuel storage site for the Ministry of Works, and then a private timber products siding. The connection to these was lifted in 1962.

Charlie Nicholas, an LMS porter at Eardisley,
c. 1940. He is sitting on the GWR travelling safe,
which provided security when cash needed to be moved
up and down the K&ER line.

Staff at Almeley, GWR, previously the Kington & Eardisley Railway, early 1930s.

GWR 0–6–0ST stands at the Midland Railway's Eardisley station, *c.* 1910. It was the train engine for the Kington & Eardisley line at the time.

Eardisley Junction, looking towards Brecon, *c.* 1950. The branch to Kington veers off to the left opposite the Midland Railway-style signal-box.

Lyonshall station, 1932. This view looks towards Almeley, eight years before the line closed. A substantial groundframe box similar to that at Almeley was positioned on the right of this photo. Between the box and the loading gauge, some open wagons can be seen in a siding, of which there were two: one Up, one Down. The ornate station was built on an embankment, so it had an entrance below platform level.

Some of the staff pose for the camera in front of the GWR station name-board at Titley Junction immediately prior to the First World War. Centre is Jack Sankey, signalman of the day, whose son, Arthur, progressed through the ranks to become a top link driver with the GWR and BR(W).

Almeley, looking towards Eardisley, *c.* 1930. The stone-built station is close to the route of the Kington Tramway, but at some distance from the village whose name it bears. It was busy conveying war-wounded veterans after 1922, following the establishment of a nearby sanatorium in the aftermath of the First World War. At the inspection of the line in July 1874, alterations were required at Almeley before it could be opened. The siding to the left has been reduced from a one-time crossing loop. A small lock-up shed on the platform is the only covered goods storage facility, but sidings to the right show a consignment of cordwood awaiting loading by mobile crane. A box containing groundframes can be seen where the line sweeps around a curve towards Eardisley. A permanent way hut lies at the end of the platform. Four passenger trains each way called at Almeley on weekdays in 1875. At the restoration of the line in 1922, the service had diminished to three each way per weekday, two of which ran as mixed trains.

Two girls smile for the camera on Almeley station, *c.* 1930.

Ex-GWR '57XX' class 0–6–0PT No. 4657 arrives at Titley Junction on a local goods run from Stanner and New Radnor, June 1951. Access to the goods siding layout to the left dates from extensions and alterations in 1902 which also brought about a replacement signal-box at the Presteign Junction end of the station. (Clayton)

Marston Halt, looking toward Pembridge, c. 1932. Another of the halts in Herefordshire opened by the GWR in 1929 to compete with local buses, this one was positioned just on the Pembridge side of the junction to Presteign. There had been a station on this site previously, which closed in 1864. Latterly, a short siding provided a minimal goods facility.

A DMU approaches Leominster and the A49 level-crossing, close to the position of Kington Junction signal box, 1964. The stub end of the Kington branch line can be seen to the left, the junction having only recently been taken out. The crossing had its gates replaced with automatic half-barriers in 1966, and changed its name from Kington to Leominster Crossing in 1970. (Hatton)

A view taken from Sunset Bridge at the New Radnor end of Kington station, c. 1920. In the distance, the signal-box of 1904 can be seen, and to the left a water tank. To the right is a spacious goods shed, an office for coal merchants Messrs Fryer – a grounded carriage body which replaced an even older one, possibly dating from the line's original carriage stock. In the foreground the River Arrow flows quietly under the bridge on this occasion, but in times of flood it frequently caused mayhem in the station area. The tall post of the home signal is partly visible on the far right.

Two similar views at Kington separated by thirty years: the upper view is from *c.* 1920, and the lower is from 1950. Both show the site of the original terminus looking towards Titley, with the second station to the left. Beyond the station building (closed in 1875) lay the cattle dock and goods shed, built by 1876. The ground to the right was once occupied by a section of the original Kington Tramway.

A closer view of the original Kington station building, looking towards Titley, *c.* 1920.

A shed to house two locomotives provided west of Kington station in about 1876 is seen here just before closure on 5 February 1951, when passenger traffic between Leominster and Kington ended. The sharp curve made by the running line required a permanent speed restriction. The prolific allotments on the left are inside the railway fence, and no doubt were tended with great care by the local staff. Kington was one of Hereford's sub-sheds.

Titley Junction, looking towards the Eardisley branch, c. 1930. The branch was removed in October 1940. The signal-box was new in 1902, replacing an earlier one, and did not close until 1958.

Kington station yard, c. 1961. Ex-GWR '14XX' class 0–4–2T No. 1420 prepares to deal with what little goods traffic remains. The coal pile looks good for a while yet, but the passenger side of the railings has been abandoned, and nature is reclaiming the goods yard, too. One station track remains as far as the end of the branch, just beyond the platform, while the other running line was removed in 1960. (B. Ashworth)

Titley Junction, looking towards Leominster, June 1951. The stub of the Eardisley Junction branch is to the right. A signal with a route indicator is a rare sight on Herefordshire branches, but the home starter shows one on this photograph. (Clayton)

Kingsland station, facing Pembridge, showing the end of the goods shed, c. 1910. This midday scene shows a flurry of activity as a passenger train, including a clerestory coach, waits at the single platform. The train token is leaning against the nearest flower tub.

Kingsland station, looking along the line to Leominster where the easy gradients across Shobdon Marsh from Pembridge continued as the line entered the Lugg valley, *c.* 1910. The signal-box of 1902 is on the left. The L&KR did not skimp on the dimensions of their station accommodation. Kingsland station was massive in proportion to the amount of traffic that derived from the locality. The signal-box replaced an earlier one in 1902, and was closed in August 1958. During the First World War the Board of Trade had an extra siding laid in Kingsland goods yard, in order to speed the reception of timber that was urgently needed for trench construction in France and Belgium. Later, Kingsland Saw Mills Ltd signed a private agreement with the GWR for the use of these sidings, which were shunted by a rope attached to a locomotive on a nearby track.

Pembridge, facing New Radnor, 1932. There is only one platform, but there were substantial brick-built offices, accommodation and a goods shed. The 'A' signal-box is on the right. This and the 'B' box by the level-crossing at the Leominster end of the station replaced one on the platform in about 1901. The 'A' box closed in 1926, leaving the 'B' box on its own until 1958, when a loop became the main line.

Pembridge station in the River Arrow valley, from the road entrance, July 1959. Passenger trains had ceased running on 7 February 1955. (H.C. Casserley)

Forge Crossing Halt, facing Presteign, with the crossing keeper in action, late 1950s. A groundframe is situated just beyond the crossing gates. This halt on the 5½ mile branch from Titley Junction to Presteign was opened on 9 March 1929, and closed to all traffic in 1964.

# CHAPTER SEVEN

# NEWPORT, ABERGAVENNY & HEREFORD RAILWAY

*A quiet time at Hereford Barton, early 1930s. In 1921 the shed was allocated forty locomotives, of which fourteen were GWR 4–4–0 types. By 1934, fourteen of these 4–4–0s were still there, though the total shed allocation had dropped to thirty-one. In 1947 the staff were responsible for fifty-two GWR locomotives, which at the time included one 4–6–0 'Castle' class, No. 4079. The shed was opened by the NA&HR in 1854, and closed over the months of November and December 1964, by which time the shed code was 86C, and the allocation consisted of: '16XX' class 0–6–0PT Nos 1613/31/57/67, '2251' class 0–6–0 Nos 2242/87, '51XX' class 2–6–2T Nos 4107/61, and '57XX' class 0–6–0PT Nos 4643/68. The last 4–6–0 locomotive to be allocated was appropriately No. 7022* Hereford Castle, *which left the shed in April 1964.*

The NA&HR was another railway with part of its route in Herefordshire that had its origin in the Welsh Midland Railway scheme of the 1840s. However, while the Welsh Midland trunk route failed, the branch line that was the NA&HR managed to muster enough support to obtain an Act of Parliament. Their Act of 1846 involved the NA&HR buying out the three companies that operated the horse-drawn Hereford & Abergavenny Tramroad, and using several stretches of this trackbed for re-laying to Pontrilas and beyond.

With Barton station as its terminus in Herford, bridging the River Wye was the only major engineering problem within the county boundary, unlike the huge works such as the Crumlin Viaduct further on into Wales.

From the opening on 2 January 1854, the NA&HR was never satisfactorily in control of its own destiny. As the money markets declined, the company fell in and out of co-operation with the LNWR over the running of its line, and had to borrow first locomotives, then rolling stock, to maintain services. An anticipated outlet via the Worcester & Hereford Railway did not materialize as quickly as expected, which left only the S&HR as a connection with the main railway network of the time. The situation began to be resolved from 1860, when the NA&HR became the western extension of a consortium of hitherto local railways under the title of the West Midland Railway.

Over the next two decades the GWR was to exert an influence in various ways that elevated the NA&HR into an integral part of an important cross-country main line. Although the 'and Newport' appeared in its original title, not until the GWR's gauge conversion in South Wales and the opening of the GWR's line from Pontypool Road to Newport in 1874 was a Birmingham–Cardiff via Hereford passenger service able to operate and vastly increase the goods traffic through to the West Midlands.

However, the LNWR still had influence. The S&HR had become joint property, shared between the GWR and LNWR, with the LNWR having running powers to Pontypool Road station and then later through to Newport. The London North Western also encouraged the development of Barrs Court as the main passenger station for Hereford.

The next major change in usage of the NA&HR came in September 1886, when the opening of the Severn Tunnel introduced the concept of the North & West main line, and enabled the development of express passenger routes which by 1892 had extended south-west to Plymouth and Penzance and north-east to Glasgow and Edinburgh. Overnight passenger services ran, and through coaches belonging to a variety of companies 'from everywhere to everywhere' were the order of the day.

During the First World War the North & West route became vital for coaling Britain's navy in its northern ports, and despite the initiatives of through train operations, the scale of traffic in goods, particularly coal, was paramount to the LMS and GWR until the last years of steam haulage under BR(W).

In the 1960s and '70s the NA&HR route in Herefordshire mirrored the experience of the S&HR line from Hereford to the north: closure of intermediate stations and a rundown in status, followed by a revitalization in both freight and passenger traffic from 1984 and on into the 1990s.

Barton station, Hereford, where the chief works and offices of the NA&HR were set up. An MR '50' class 2–4–0 in original condition is facing south, with the Whitecross road bridge in the background. The date is uncertain, but it could be 1869, when the MR began working Brecon trains into Barton, or about 1874, when the MR resumed using Barton again after a dispute with the GWR. The first three carriages belong to the MR, and luggage is carried on the roof in 'stagecoach' style. The second carriage from the engine is first class in the middle and second class at either end, for the servants. The first and third carriages are third class, where passengers sat on wooden benches with low back partitions so that the light from the oil lamps was available for the whole carriage.

Red Hill Junction signal-box replaced an earlier one in 1927, and closed on 31 July 1966, when the junction was taken out of use. The 2 mile 10 chain Rotherwas–Red Hill line was laid in 1864 by the LNWR as a means of re-routing GWR passenger traffic from the south into Barrs Court station to connect with that of the LNWR.

Hereford Barton yard, looking towards Red Hill Junction, c. 1932. The running sheds lie behind Barton signal-box on the right. To the left of the sidings where a GWR Pannier tank is shunting, the left-curving track led to a private siding leading to the flour mill of Messrs Watkins Bros.

Demolition of Barton station, c. November 1913. Barton station had become surplus to requirements, and was closed on 2 January 1893. The West Midland Railway, formed in 1860, which included the NA&HR and W&HR, was absorbed by the GWR in 1863, and consequently all GWR services except the Gloucester line were then using Barton station. This left the LNWR isolated with a dead end at Barrs Court. To counteract this situation, the LNWR put in Red Hill Junction, and the GWR started to run into Barrs Court. Later, the Barton and Brecon Curve opened on 1 January 1893, leaving Barton station without the Brecon line passenger trains.

'Modified Hall' class 4–6–0 No. 6999 *Capel Dewi Hall* approaches the level-crossing at the Tram Inn under the watchful eye of the signalman in the box (opened 1894), *c.* 1955. The train is a stopper to Cardiff from Hereford. At the time the crossover in view led to a goods shed and sidings, which were retained for traffic until 5 October 1964. The name 'Tram Inn' is a reminder of the fact that in parts the N&HR was constructed on top of the trackbed of the horse-drawn tramway which opened for traffic on 21 September 1829.

EWS Type 4 No. 47786 *Roy Castle OBE* having arrived at Pontrilas siding with the first delivery of timber from Arrochar near Loch Lomond, via Newport, 24 June 1997. This joint initiative between EWS and Pontrilas Timber and Builders' Merchants was the first regular use of the siding since closure to goods in 1964, and has since led to an extension being laid in August 1997. (Hereford Times)

Pontrilas station, looking towards Hereford, with a GWR 0–6–0 tender goods engine by the water column and the signal-box behind. The station building extension has not yet taken place, and a wooden shelter on the Down platform pre-dates a later brick-built version. The porters nearest the camera still have numbered armbands, which were dispensed with from 1902. The two staff behind with buttoned-up jackets are wearing the uniform of the ticket collector grades.

A view taken from the Barton Road bridge looking towards Whitecross road bridge, August 1958. A '2251' class 0–6–0 crosses the site where Sainsbury's supermarket was later built. Barton shed is to the left, and closed between 2 November and December 1964. The line the locomotive is travelling from Red Hill Junction was taken out of use on 31 July 1966, and the yard became a dead end until it also ceased work on 29 October 1979. The position of the old NA&HR Barton station is beyond the lines of open wagons to the right.

Ex-GWR 0–6–0 No. 2256, one of the original 1930 batch of C.B. Collett's successful design, stands in woebegone condition in Barton yard, August 1961. No. 2256 was to last just over a year more before being condemned in September 1962. There were still four of this class available at Barton shed in the summer of 1964, the year of closure. Among their work were the Brecon line passenger and goods trains when that line was in its last years, and the class ran the final services over the Ross line.

Barton shed, looking west, c. 1920. The locomotives, including two 0–6–0 saddle tanks, are awaiting entry to the fitting shop beyond the hoist. The open wagon standing alongside the coal dump belongs to the Hull & Barnsley Railway. Eventually, Barton shed housed all locomotives based in Hereford, and was home at various times prior to nationalization to GWR, LMS and even LNER 'J25' class 0–6–0s on loan during the Second World War. Standard BR classes appeared before the shed closed to steam in December 1964. Barton also serviced the sub-sheds at Kington, Ledbury, Leominster and Ross until they each became redundant.

St Devereux for Kilpeck station, looking towards Hereford, April 1958, just prior to closure to all traffic on 9 June 1958. A signal-box, closed in 1959, stood out of camera view to the left. The platforms had been extended since the station opened. (R. Casserley)

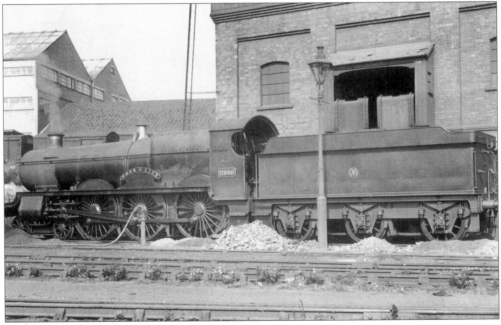

GWR 29XX 'Saint' class 4–6–0 No. 2980 *Coeur de Lion* stands alongside the coaling stage at Hereford Barton shed, 1934. The tender displays the so-called 'shirt button'-style 'GWR' of the era. No. 2980's home shed in 1934 was Gloucester, but Hereford shed always had a close association with the class, which hauled the heaviest expresses on the North & West route. A total of eight 'Saints' were among the Hereford shed allocation in 1947.

# CHAPTER EIGHT

# WORCESTER, BROMYARD & LEOMINSTER RAILWAY

*An ex-GWR 0–6–0PT prepares to return to Worcester on the truncated service train at Bromyard station, 1961. It is standing at the only platform in public use, the original one of the first railway. At this stage the '57XX' class had a monopoly of all the workings along the route. Behind the locomotive is the signal-box, and behind that part of the goods yard, with large sheds belonging to an animal foodstuff and agricultural merchant. By their decision to close the line beyond Bromyard, the Railway Executive returned this station to its original designation as a terminus.*

Public recognition of the need for a railway to connect Worcester to Leominster via Bromyard surfaced in 1845 with plans by the Welsh Midland Railway to include such a line as a branch of their main line across Central Wales to the coast. As with most proposals of the next decade, Herefordshire was viewed as a pathway to South Wales from the Midlands, particularly for goods traffic, rather than as a district likely to produce great revenue internally. The link from Bransford Road on the W&HR Malvern line to Leominster on the S&HR line was considered as yet another possibility for a major company to tap the South Wales coal trade.

However, finances continued to be raised locally, and the support of the county's landowners was paramount. A provisional committee, including some directors of the newly formed West Midland Railway, met in 1860 to oversee a parliamentary application which led to the Worcester, Bromyard & Leominster Act of 1 August 1861.

Although sufficient money had been underwritten to anticipate rapid development, when the calls to pay up came, little was forthcoming, and it was not until October 1864 that a construction contract was let. Then began a series of frustrating difficulties with contractors. The first went bankrupt in 1866, the second was insolvent by January 1867, and the original company was then surprisingly re-hired, but failed to complete the task before a fourth contractor finally finished the job. Subsequently, appeals were advertised for more local money, and also to the GWR to come to the aid of the ailing company with a working agreement. Neither materialized, so abandonment of the section beyond Bromyard was approved by the Board of Trade in 1869, and only then did the GWR agree, in November 1870, to work the line in perpetuity for 52½ per cent of the gross receipts.

It was October 1877 before Bromyard had a railway station open to the public. In due course the original company was dissolved, and the line was vested in the GWR from 1 July 1888.

While the WL&BR struggled, another unconnected company had received an Act on 30 July 1874 to complete the through route onwards from Bromyard to Leominster, over slightly more difficult terrain in comparison to the section from Worcester, and progress was made at much the same slow rate as its counterpart. Eventually, the construction contract only as far as Steens Bridge from Leominster (3½ miles) was let in 1880, and even on completion of this stretch, arguments over the access to Leominster station caused yet more delay until 1884.

Not until thirty-six years after its initial Act was the whole line completed, and even then it took the GWR to complete the task, having taken over the L&BR in 1888.

Finally, on 1 September 1897, North Herefordshire had its railway link to Worcester in place. A proposed direct rail link from Bromyard to Hereford had fallen out of favour, and no through route across Central Wales ever came into being.

Agricultural traffic, particularly from Bromyard market, with the hop trade and fruit growers, kept the line busy until the advent of the livestock lorry and road milk tanker began the erosion of this income. Not a highly populated region anyway, of all the intermediate stations on the branch only Bromyard was sited close to any significant numbers of potential customers, and when the country bus service routes developed, the GWR, and later BR, had to compete by offering various reduced-price excursions to make up some of its lost daily passenger revenue.

After years of declining income, the Bromyard–Leominster section was closed by the Railway Executive on 15 September 1952. Even the economies of diesel railcars for passenger services could not save the remaining Worcester–Bromyard section of the line, and although delayed for a while, it eventually closed on 5 September 1964. Some passenger services continued beyond Leominster to Kington and New Radnor.

Leominster sub-shed was responsible for many duties on the line until it was truncated at Bromyard, and the usual locomotives in operation were '517' and '3571' class 0–4–2Ts, followed from the 1930s by the '48XX' updated equivalent 0–4–2Ts. Later still, the '57XX' 0–6–0PTs were allowed over the line from 1940 onwards. Goods workings were in the hands of the lighter classes of 0–6–0 saddle and pannier tanks, 'Dean Goods' and then '2251' class 0–6–0 tender engines.

The last effort to capture some passenger traffic between Worcester (Shrub Hill) and Bromyard was to use a single-coach DMU, seen here at Bromyard, 1964. Bromyard was then the terminus, with only the platform in view used by passengers – and even here paving slabs had been lifted to restrict access.

Looking towards Leominster, a fine crop of lupins sprouts from the shortened Down platform just prior to total closure at Bromyard, June 1964. Ex-GWR '57XX' class 0–6–0PT No. 4664 has brought in a short goods train from Worcester sidings. Beyond the overbridge at 135 miles 30 chains there was a stopblock terminating the route. (B. Ashworth)

The line between Leominster and Bromyard had been closed for six years when the Stephenson Railway Society asked the Western Region of BR to run a special trip along the line for their members in April 1958. In this view, looking toward Fencote, the special, hauled by 2–6–2T No. 4571, is approaching Bromyard, passing below the footbridge by the tilerie which once had a world-wide trade in its products, connected to the rail network through a short exchange siding.

A view of Bromyard station taken from a high vantage point in St Peter's Church, c. 1910. The Bromyard Downs feature on the skyline, with a cricket match in progress on one field, and a pony and trap waits for custom at the lower end of the station drive. The station yard and the Broad Bridge road were remodelled in 1897, when Bromyard ceased to be a terminus and the through route (left) to Leominster opened. The goods yard, once the site of a wooden engine shed, contains coal stacks and lengths of round timber, with a travelling crane to assist in loading.

Mrs Esme Halford on the steps of Fencote signal-box, *c.* 1945. Mrs Halford represents a number of women throughout Herefordshire who came forward during the Second World War to help overcome the shortage of railway staff. She shared the signalling duty shifts with her husband, Fred, from 1941 until the end of the war. A whitewash brush hangs on the wall ready for use: to avoid aiding enemy planes by the use of lighting, many hazards around the station were regularly painted white during the wartime blackout.

Fencote station, a view through the road overbridge towards Leominster, *c.* 1958, after the siding track on the left had been lifted. The GWR Type 7 signal-box of 1897, with twenty-three levers, controlled the 950 ft long crossing loop in the station, along with a short siding behind a goods shed, out of view to the right. William Clarke designed the attractive station buildings, which survive in preservation, as do those at the next station towards Leominster, at Rowden Mill. Traffic ceased from 15 September 1952 through Fencote, which was noted as having the highest altitude of any station in Herefordshire.

The auction of the Bromyard station furniture is about to take place in 1964, and viewing is in progress. The event does not appear to have created much interest, judging by the small number of people present. They are standing on the platform created in the 1897 extension to Leominster, and the view looks in this direction. The concrete agricultural stores buildings in the background were a late addition to the goods facilities in the yard.

'The Railway Children' from nearby Lower Nicholson Farm in Foxholes cutting, *c.* 1939. This is the site where unexpectedly hard rock brought problems and delays during construction work between Steens Bridge and Bromyard in the mid-1890s. Like many line-side residents on the rural branch lines, the Phillips family had close connections with the railway and its employees. Unofficial deliveries of goods such as newspapers were made from the train in exchange for farm produce such as eggs. (Via J. Phillips)

# CHAPTER NINE

# OTHER RAILWAYS

*GWR 0–6–0PT No. 3788 of Ludlow sub-shed passes Easton Court station with the 3.5 p.m. Tenbury Wells–Ludlow Joint Railway freight, 20 October 1939. Behind the station lies the Easton Court estate, the Tenbury road, the station entrance, and also a small siding controlled by a groundframe which was added by 1920. The station closed on 31 July 1961, along with the Woofferton–Tenbury Wells section of the route, which ran on much of the bed of the aborted Kington, Leominster & Stourport Canal when constructed. (S.H.P. Higgins)*

For most of its length, the Tenbury & Bewdley Railway was situated in Worcestershire and Shropshire, but a very short section of its route was on Herefordshire soil, around Easton Court – 'for Little Hereford', as the station name-board later had added to its main title.

In addition to what might be termed the public sector railway network in Herefordshire, there have been a number of other sites and systems of interest. For a number of years railway preservation enthusiasts had the use of private sidings at H.P. Bulmer Ltd, Moorfields, where various groups could store and work upon locomotives and other rolling stock, and where servicing could be carried out by support teams on locomotives involved in main line specials that were routed through Barrs Court.

Two neighbouring stations on the Bromyard branch, Rowden Mill and Fencote, have been saved to remind visitors of bygone railway days, each featuring items of rolling stock to enhance the environment. Titley Junction station has undergone some restoration, as has the goods shed at Ross-on-Wye. Eardisley station building was transported to Welshpool as part of a preservation project. Other artefacts remain in alternative uses: Hay goods shed is a farm supplies warehouse, Ross engine shed is an antiques mart, Bromyard station site is in use as a narrow gauge passenger line's terminus, and several stations have gone into private hands, for holiday accommodation at Pontrilas, a private house at St Devereux, and a car sales office at Tram Inn.

By their nature, Herefordshire's rail-linked military depots were forbidden to photographers, so Credenhill and Rotherwas from the First World War and Moreton-on-Lugg, Pontrilas and Rotherwas from the Second World War are almost impossible to represent. Purely industrial railways in Herefordshire were few and of short length and lifespan, and were usually involved with the extracting industries, or were contractors' lines at the time of construction.

Easton Court station opened to passengers and goods in August 1861, closed in October 1862, and then reopened in April 1865. The station was built as a concession to Sir Joseph Bailey, the Lord of the Manor, whose home was Easton Court. The nearby hamlet of Little Hereford had its name added to the station's in November 1889. In this view, *c.* 1902, the bunting and flags indicate a special day, with the station-master on the platform and the young porter peeping from the door.

The designation 'ROF No. 1' can just be read on the bunker of this Kerr, Stuart and Co. Ltd 0–6–0T which was delivered new to the Ministry of Munitions depot at Rotherwas in 1916. It is seen here having been sold as surplus to requirements and under new ownership. Rotherwas depot finally closed in September 1966, and rail traffic ceased from that date. (IRS)

From 1968 until October 1993 the Bulmer Railway Centre at Moorfields, Hereford, played host to the preserved railway vehicles of a number of organizations, and also acted as an important service point for steam locomotives hauling main line specials. The 6000 Locomotive Association took delivery of the Peckett 0–4–0ST on 1 March 1972, and it was later named *Pectin* in 1974. Here, a brake van contains passengers as the short train moves around the curve at Moorfields.

Painter Bros Ltd introduced locomotives for duties on part of their 2 ft gauge tramway system, which was situated adjacent to the standard gauge sidings inside the premises at Mortimer Road, Hereford. Here, a Lister Blackstone Traction Ltd four-wheel diesel mechanical unit moves some galvanized components around.

The WD insignia is seen on the cab of the Fowler & Co. 0–4–0 diesel mechanical on its way in a goods train to be delivered to ROF Elm Bridge via Pontrilas, 1941.

Ex-GWR 'King' class 4–6–0 No. 6000 *King George V* stands outside Barrs Court station while photographers happily record the historic moment on 2 October 1971, when steam was allowed out on the main line again after a campaign led by Mr Peter Prior against a ban that had lasted three years. On the left, the Engineers Department has taken over most of the siding space. To the front is the College Road bridge, which replaced a level-crossing in the 1870s, and a sign of updating of the signalling with colour lights is in view.

Rowden Mill station was restored from dereliction over a period up to 1984 under the direction of John Wilkinson, and very quickly achieved recognition, receiving British Rail's Heritage Award in 1989. Several preserved items of rolling stock can be found on site. In this view, a GWR inspection saloon, No. W80976, is visible.

# BIBLIOGRAPHY

*History of the GWR*, E.T. McDermot, revised by C.R. Clinker (Ian Allan)

*The West Midland Lines of the GWR*, K.M. Black (Ian Allan)

*Early Railways between Hereford and Abergavenny*, Cook and Clinker (RC&HS)

*The Hay and Kington Railway*, Rattenbury and Clinker (RC&HS)

*Track Layout Diagrams of the GWR*, R.A. Cooke (Cooke)

*The Facility of Locomotion, The Kington Railways*, Sinclair and Fenn (Mid Border/Caradoc Books)

*The Golden Valley Railway*, W.H. Smith (Wild Swan Publications)

*Rails Through the Hills*, J. Boynton (Mid England Books)

*Railway Observer* (RCTS)

*Locomotives of the GWR* (RCTS)

*Great Western Way* (HMRS)

*British Railway Journal* (Wild Swan Publications)

*HMRS Journal*

*GWR Locomotive Allocations, 1921 and 1934*, Harrison and Pocock (Wild Swan Publications)

*BR Steam Shed Allocations, Pt 2*, P.B. Hands (Defiant Publications)